BURNING
BUSH
2.0
HOW
POP CULTURE
REPLACED
THE
PROPHET

PAUL ASAY

ABINGDON PRESS
NASHVILLE

BURNING BUSH 2.0
HOW POP CULTURE REPLACED THE PROPHET

Copyright © 2015 by Paul Asay

All rights reserved.

Library of Congress Cataloging-in-Publication Data

Asay, Paul.
  Burning bush 2.0 : how pop culture replaced the prophet / Paul Asay.
    pages cm
  ISBN 978-1-4267-8741-6 (binding: soft back) 1. Popular culture—Religious aspects—Christianity. 2. Christianity and culture. 3. Christianity—21st century. I. Title.
  BR115.C8A83 2015
  261—dc23

2015004185

15 16 17 18 19 20 21 22 23 24—10 9 8 7 6 5 4 3 2 1

MANUFACTURED IN THE UNITED STATES OF AMERICA

This book is dedicated to Wendy,
who has loved and supported me through twenty-five years
of good times and bad, through sickness and health,
through newspapers and ministries and all too many deadlines.
Thanks for everything you've put up with, everything you do,
and everything you are. I love you.

CONTENTS

CONTENTS

INTRODUCTION

Once upon a time . . .

Every story begins as such, whether it says so or not. Whether the first words are "In the beginning" or "Call me Ishmael" or "A long time ago in a galaxy far, far away," the promise of *once upon a time* is there. It's both the invitation and invocation of storytelling, a hot cup of tea and a fasten-your-seatbelt sign. *You're going away for a while,* those four words promise. *Prepare to find yourself in a different place, a different time, perhaps a different world. We've got a story to share.*

When I was about four, my dad told me my first story—or, at least, the first I remember. I sat on his lap and leaned against his chest, mesmerized.

Once upon a time, there was a boy named Paul, this story began.

Already, I knew it was going to be the best story ever. And it went something like this.

Once upon a time, there was a boy named Paul, and he had a friend named Big Bird (the *Sesame Street character,* but more important, a stuffed animal I slept with every night). *One day, Paul and Big Bird were walking down the street, when suddenly (!) a big, black dog leapt out from a dark alleyway! He had huge eyes and white, shiny teeth, and he growled a low, terrible growl: Grrrrrrr!... Big Bird was scared. He was so scared that he opened his mouth, turned around, and ran away, as fast as his big orange feet could carry him. But dogs, they're faster than big birds, and people too. They love to chase things. And a big dog like that, if it caught up to Big Bird, who knows what might happen. But just when that big, black dog was about to run after Big Bird, growling and barking, POP! Paul hit it right on the nose. And that big, black dog ran away.*

It was the perfect story. It had everything a four-year-old could want: horror, action, comedy, and a brave, bold hero. And then the ultimate kicker: that hero was me! Maybe not the me sitting with my dad at that moment. Both he and I knew full well he'd never let me and a suddenly self-aware stuffed animal walk down a street unsupervised. We both knew it was pretend. But the Paul in that story—the hero—was the kind of boy I wanted to be someday: brave, courageous, and willing to go out of his way to help those weaker and more cowardly than himself. Sure, maybe in truth I was a little more like Big Bird than Paul, prone to running away from big, scary dogs (or worse, sitting down and crying). But the story gave me a vision of myself that I'm not sure that I truly had before.

And when I look at the stories I still love to this day, they all have elements of that very first story. I no longer listen to them on my father's lap. I read about them, watch them, listen to them, and play them. Sure, the characters are different: Big Bird might be a damsel in distress or a couple of kids trapped in a burning building or the whole universe. The scary dog might be a demon or drug lord or the vacuum of space. The hero might carry a Bata-rang or a magic ring or simply the courage of his convictions. And none of these stories mentions me by name.

And yet many of them are, in their own way, still all about me. About who I am. How I feel. Who I fear I might become. Who I want to be someday.

Stories are always about us. That's why they move us so.

Think about it: People talk about their jobs and say, "It's just like *Office Space*." Or they compare one of their friends to Shel-don from *The Big Bang Theory*. Couples turn love ballads into "our song," and when they break up, someone will invariably play the same emo tune again and again and again. Video games are the apex of self-focused storytelling in some ways, where we become for a time a different person onscreen, able to slay dragons or beat Bowser— a little like a four-year-old boy was able to punch a big, black dog in the nose.

Through our heroes and villains, we see pieces of us. We slip into the narrative as we slip through a door, entering a new world where we can root for our heroes and feel their hardships. When the characters suffer, we wince. We look away. We grow angry. Sometimes we cry. I know *I* do, anyway.

Yeah, these characters may be pure fiction—the product of a fertile imagination somewhere in London or Los Angeles or Lub-bock, Texas. But they can feel so real, so powerful. And through them, we often discover who we are and who we'd like to be.

The words *once upon a time* can take us to centuries past or to the future, to epochs that never have been or might one day be. They whisk us across the street or the world or the galaxy. But the best stories show us places in ourselves too—trips through our minds and our psyches and our very souls. Stories are, by their very nature, *spiritual*. They can play around with our intellect, tossing out ideas and theories and quandaries to puzzle over and then go deeper. They can knead our emotions, triggering laughter and fear and sadness and joy, and then go deeper. They dive to the very core of our being, expressing thoughts and feelings that, before we saw or heard the story, had no real words. We find the dissonance between our fallen world and God's glorious blueprint, the deep, voiceless longing we have for justice and mercy and grace and love.

In our stories, we look for God, even if we don't know it. And sometimes, I believe, we find a hint of him. An echo, perhaps. A fingerprint. We're swallowed by the story and feel God in the ribs. We bathe in the story and emerge, clean and dripping, through a sense of God's grace. We walk through a story—one that can feel desolate and dry and forsaken—and happen upon a strange, unexpected bush, flames twining its branches like fingers through hair. We feel a little like Moses, standing in front of something familiar yet transcendent. And we, like Moses, find ourselves on holy ground.

Our stories speak of who we are. Who we've become. And who God has always wanted us to be.

Over the last several years, I've spent a lot of time thinking about the power of story—especially through films and television shows and songs and video games. As a critic for an organization called *Plugged In* (a Christian website that reviews all of that stuff and more), it's been my job. And while much of that time has been spent talking about how stories can impact us negatively (which they can), this book will look at our entertainment in a different way: as a conduit for something better.

A couple of cautions are in order before I go any further. First, be warned that, as I discuss some of culture's popular movies, television shows, music, and even video games, I'll be getting into some spoilers. *Lots* of spoilers. It's unfortunate but unavoidable, considering how deeply we need to delve into some of this stuff. So if I start talking about, say, a movie you've always meant to see but haven't yet, don't feel bad about skipping forward a bit. I won't take offense. Just be sure to come back later so we can catch up on thinking through and talking about some of the important issues and questions that arise; that is, after all, the main point.

Second, and just as important, don't take anything I say here as an excuse to see something that you might otherwise avoid. I'll explain what I mean in more detail later and then again near the end of the book. Taking entertainment—including some really problematic entertainment—and trying to suss out the "better" from it is inherently controversial, and I get that. I'm expecting picketers to show up at my house at any minute. We Christians have always had a really strange relationship with art, entertainment, and story itself—I think in part because we know how powerful these elements can be. As any expendable henchman in a James Bond movie could tell you, power that falls into the wrong hands can be really dangerous.

But as I'll explain more in the next chapter, I don't think God really restricts himself to speaking just through church-produced films and CCM artists. We know Jesus hung out with prostitutes and tax collectors because those are the folks who most needed him. He wasn't worried about his message being compromised by rubbing elbows with society's unsavory elements. And honestly, I don't think God worries about that either. He knows who needs to hear from him the most, and it's probably not the mom who owns every Chris Tomlin album ever, including the bootleg tapes.

I think God's a natural storyteller. The Bible is part of the story he tells us. And guess what? Even though the characters in it lived thousands of years ago and are named Habakkuk and Gomer and Jehoshaphat, the book is still all about us—about our shame and hope, our rocky past, and, if we choose, our glorious future.

God's storytelling ways give me hope for heaven.

Most Christians, I think, imagine the realm beyond those pearly gates as the ultimate *happily ever after*—the inevitable bookend to the *once upon a time* beginning. It's the payoff for all the strife and hardship we've experienced, a place where every street is golden and every house has granite countertops and everyone's favorite sports team always wins the championship.

Maybe this shows that I'm sadly stunted, spiritually speaking, but that sounds kinda boring to me. I mean, I like granite countertops as much as the next guy, and it sure would be nice to see the Colorado Rockies win someday. But in the best of stories, the worst part is invariably the end.

And God, I think, understands this. He understands why we love our stories, and that we need our share of Big Birds to save and scary dogs to punch in the nose. He wired us that way, after all, and either he'll see to our rewiring or give us some fun and exciting things for us to do. And even though up there in heaven we'll be the people God always wanted us to be, finally free of all that sin and fallenness, I'd like to think we'd still be able to learn and grow, to be a part of some new, exciting, and beautiful stories.

For me, I'd rather look at heaven not as a glorious conclusion, but as an exciting beginning. It's not the ultimate *happily ever after*. It's the promise of an eternity of new adventures. The ultimate *once upon a time*.

CHAPTER 1
PROPHETABLE ENTERPRISE

God Doesn't Speak Just Through Robed,
Bearded Guys Anymore

The Universe is made of stories, not of atoms.
—Muriel Rukeyser, *The Speed of Darkness: Poems*

I t's tough to be a prophet.

It wasn't always so. Back in the day, prophets—real, bona fide, Old Testament prophets—commanded respect. No one cared that they dressed funny. No one made fun of their hipster beards. Never mind that they rarely had much good to say—people would still (mostly) listen to them: kings would beg for private audiences, the rich and powerful would plead for insight. Prophets could change national policy or upend a country's very soul.

They were, in short, a lot like economists. Which might explain their shared affinity for beards.

But while economists are still widely respected, folks who claim to hear directly from God—like, through awesome cell phone service or something—don't get a lot of traction these days. Dress in sackcloth, and you'll be directed to the nearest Old Navy. Snack on locusts, and, unless you're living in a truly cutting-edge neighborhood in New York or L.A., you'll just gross people out. Visions and messages from God are things you talk about with your psychologist, not proclaim to the world. In some ways, yesterday'sprophet would seem to be today's homeless schizophrenic.

This is not to invalidate the messages of Old Testament prophets. It's just that—well, times have changed. We've changed. We're not the same people who spent most of our waking lives farming and shepherding and stoning the occasional infidel. We've got the Internet to occupy our time now. Smartphones. Netflix. In a world filled with a million LOLcats and where "following" someone is a matter of clicking a button, a loud guy with ashes on his head wouldn't be worth a dozen YouTube views. We see way weirder, more seemingly relevant stuff on our Facebook feeds. Burning bush? You need an *exploding* bush to get someone's attention.

But God still wants to talk with us. And it's not like he's the sort to get stuck on just one form of communication. While the prophet might've been his go-to mode of dialogue for a millennium or two, God has spoken through other means as well: through dreams and visions, through singing angels and talking donkeys, through scrolls and books and stone tablets and scratches on the palace wall. God is remarkably versatile when he wants our attention. He knows we're not capable of communicating on his level. So he bends down and talks to us on ours.

So if screaming prophets are a bit passé now, how does God communicate with us in the twenty-first century? Through the very same tools we use to communicate truth and beauty and pain and everything else worth talking about: through music, through movies and television shows, through words written and spoken and sung.

Oh, I don't think he's abandoned the traditional prophetic route; he'll play that card when it best serves his purpose. But mostly, I think God talks to us through channels with which we're familiar, using a technique he knows we've always been particularly receptive to.

He speaks to us through story.

STORYTIME

When I was a teeny kid, I'd climb into my mommy's lap and force her to read to me. I'd carry a whole bunch of books in my arms, plop them beside us on the couch, and we'd start going through them, one by one. Sometimes they were books with lots of pictures and very few words. *Are You My Mother?* by P. D. Eastman and *Curious George* by Margret and H. A. Rey were particular favorites. Sometimes (just because she was that sort of mommy), she'd read something with very few pictures, which forced me to pay special attention to all the words—such as *Winnie-the-Pooh* by A. A. Milne or Rudyard Kipling's *Just So Stories*. And very often, we'd read Bible stories, either from a big, intimidating-looking book or smaller, picture-heavy paperbacks. They'd be about Jonah and the whale, or Jesus feeding five thousand people, or the good Samaritan.

I was in church and Sunday school almost all the time then too, but I don't remember a single sermon. I didn't keep a single picture I made, no matter how much macaroni I glued onto the thing. But I do remember the stories my mother read to me . . . the pictures, the feel of the heavy pages, the rise and fall of her voice.

God likes stories. He must. The Bible has a lot of stories in it—more, I'd wager, than almost any other major religious text. If you're Muslim or Buddhist, you hear a lot about what these leaders *said*. In Christianity, it's just as important what Jesus *did*—the true stories that made up his own earthly life. And even when Jesus taught, he often taught through parables, stories of poor women and prodigal sons and even mustard seeds.

And for me, story has always brought me closer to him—even when more traditional avenues of Christianity sometimes pushed me away. In junior high, when I felt awkward and alone at church, I found God by reading and rereading and rerereading C. S. Lewis's *The Chronicles of Narnia*. In college, as I was dealing with questions and doubts, I found him lurking in Fyodor Dostoyevsky's *Crime and Punishment* and speaking in Augustine's *Confessions*. When life is hard and things go wrong, I find that I want to hear a story. And God always seems to hand me one—whether it's in book or song, on big screen or small.

If a guy rushes up to me on the street and hollers, "Repent!" I'm likely to cross—quickly—to the other side (perhaps while dialing security). But stories hit a soft spot in me. When nothing seems to stick to my Teflon brain, stories have a way of worming their way inside.

And I think God doesn't just restrict himself to explicit tales of his grace or power or whatnot, where he actually lands in the credits. He's not found just in Bible narratives like *Son of God* or pretty clear allegories like Aslan in *Narnia*. He's in places we might never expect. Sometimes I think that he must be in *every* story somehow—stories told in print and picture, on our iPods and Xboxes.

What, you thought God might avoid those things? Does he have something against the Kinect?

SACRED CREATION

That's a pretty bold statement, saying that hints of God can be found in *everything*. In fact, just suggesting that would be enough to get me smacked down (perhaps literally) by many a pastor. And true, God's sometimes almost impossible to find. It's hard to feel God's presence when watching, say, a *Two and a Half Men* rerun.

But I think it might be true. Let me try to explain why, beginning at the beginning. The *very* beginning.

"And the earth was without form, and void," we're told in the first chapter of Genesis, King James Version, "and darkness was upon the face of the deep. And the Spirit of God moved upon the face of the waters. And God said, Let there be light" (vv. 2-3). Pretty fascinating, this tiny little passage: so much mystery, so little science.

Could God have given us a bevy of complex physics equations in Genesis, explaining the Big Bang and the expanding universe and the bizarre nature of dark matter and why in the heck he made the whole place so big? Probably. But I don't think that he was really interested in giving us a dry, scientific lecture. He knew that, as time went on, we'd learn more about that stuff ourselves (and, like any good father, God knew that learning is so much more satisfying if it feels like we're doing it on our own). Plus, most of us nonscientific types wouldn't have remembered much of that sort of biblical lecture anyway. (The only thing I remember from chemistry class is how quickly a Bunsen burner can set a book on fire.)

But stories stick with us. And here, in Genesis, the *how* of the universe is less important than the *who* (God) and the *why* (because it was good). And you can't get that stuff across in an equation. For that, you need something else: you need a story.

And it's really interesting that, according to Genesis, God makes the universe just like we might make a story. He *tells* it into existence. He didn't shape the light with his hands or blink it into being. He *spoke*, and it was so. In a sense, God told a story, a true story—not of something that had happened, but something *happening*, something that was *going to happen*. It's a story told in future tense—where the Narrator speaks and it comes to be.

Nifty trick, that.

An act of creation was a story. And in a sense, every story is an act of creation.

In *God in the Dock*, C. S. Lewis wrote that "miracles in fact are a retelling in small letters of the very same story which is written across the whole world in letters too large for some of us to see." But the reverse is also true. The stories *we* tell are little miracles in and of themselves—miraculous in that we're even able to tell them at all. They, more than anything else, draw the line between us and the animals, between us sentient bags of flesh and our ever-more-intelligent machines. Our stories speak of our free will. They prove our ability to reason and to express our appreciation for wonder and beauty.

When we're told that we are made in God's image, this is what I think of: our ability to craft a good story. It's not so much that we resemble God physically (although it may be that too), but that he somehow imprinted a part of who he is on our minds and spirits and souls. God speaks to us through his creation. And we, his greatest creation, were given the ability to create as well. And we don't craft these stories just in our traditional language, but in the language of picture and sculpture and music. When we create something—anything, really, even if it's a two-line "poem" that everyone including your mother hates—we surpass every other living, breathing thing on the planet, every computer ever programmed. We are telling stories. We're creating. We're reflecting, however badly, part of God's own character.

We can't just conjure up a tree from nothingness, of course, like God can. But we can make up a story about a tree from a handful of letters. We can't make a man or a mountain. But in our stories, we can make a man climb a mountain and have him do almost anything we want him to do—build a house or sing a song or find buried treasure.

I think that this act of creation—storytelling through word or song or art—is God's greatest gift to us. J. R. R. Tolkien, the author of *The Lord of the Rings*, called our storytelling an act of "sub-creation." No wonder that throughout history, some of our greatest artistic achievements have been focused on the ultimate Artist—returning a little bit of the favor, as it were.

But even if our works don't seem to be explicitly focused on God, he sneaks in sometimes, even without our permission. If we write a story about a bush, he can set it a-burning, whether we want him to or not.

GOD: LET'S TALK

They don't call it the House of Mouse for nothing.

Go to Disneyland or one of the theme parks in Walt Disney World, and you'll see Mickey Mouse everywhere. His face is plastered on shirts, ties, playing cards, and cookie tins. His ears sprout on the heads of overstimulated six-year-olds and half-ironic teens. His oversized self wanders oh-so-tidy Main Street or sits like Santa Claus in Mickey's Toontown. If you're not cheerful enough, he's likely to chase you down, shake you, and stare at you with those strangely dead eyes of his until you promise to *smile and laugh and enjoy the happiest place on earth . . . or else!*

But even when Mickey's not thrusting his black ears and nose directly into your business, he's still everywhere. Secret references to the guy are found in every Disney theme park—so many, in fact, that it's become a pastime of some true Disneyphiles to locate and catalog these "Hidden Mickeys." There's a Mickey-shaped lock on one of the treasure chests in the Pirates of the Caribbean. A skeleton wears a set of Mickey Mouse ears in the Indiana Jones Adventure ride. Mickey's image is hidden in the queue of Expedition Everest and can be found as you exit the Tower of Terror. He's probably hiding in your corn dog if you look closely enough. Nearly a thousand of these Hidden

Mickeys have been found thus far, enough to fill up books and websites and entirely too much spare time of some otherwise productive adults.

For me, finding God in entertainment is a little like those Hidden Mickeys. He's everywhere if we bother to look. It'd be almost impossible for him not to be.

We've already talked about God's creative streak—how he spoke the universe into being and how the whole thing is really just part of the impossibly awesome story he's telling. And the Bible tells us that we're the best thing he's ever done—God's own *Anna Karenina* and *Mona Lisa* and Symphony No. 7 all wrapped up in these skin wrappers of ours.

I've suggested that one of the things that makes us so great is that God has given us our *own* ability to create. Sure, our abilities are inherently a little downsized: we can't whip up star systems or a Crab Nebula. We can't even piece together an original bit of shrubbery. But when we make stories through word or song or art, we're most closely tapping into what God does—creating something out of nothing but our own mental and emotional faculties. We create sometimes to illustrate a point or touch an emotional nerve, or to express beauty or horror or wonder. We create because, on some level, we have to. It's part of our nature to express our love in this way—a love of the creation and, hopefully, a love of the one for whom we're creating it. And that desire to express love through what we make, whether it's a sonnet or a symphony or a handmade construction-paper card with macaroni glued all over it, hints, I think, at God's own (and ultimately unfathomable) desire to create: he made us because he already loved us. He made us because he wanted us to love him. And everything we see originally was designed to express and illustrate that love, to us and for us and for everything around us. Creation itself is, on some level, a great big Valentine's Day card.

So if creation is integral to God's nature, and if God—loving us as he does—passed a hint of that nature on to us, that must mean our own humble creative achievements are, in a way, sacred acts. Whether they're horrible or wonderful, whether they're meant to honor God or not, they still reflect part of his nature. Just as we were made in God's image, our creative images reflect that divine instinct to create. God created us. He gave us a desire to create too. And so, because we're all products of that master blueprint, I think that a bit of God's nature gloms onto whatever we make—a little like a Hidden Mickey. It's tucked into the pages of a book. It's lurking in the second verse of a song. It's hiding in a game's fourth level, just behind that lurching, groaning zombie you can't get by.

Sometimes we acknowledge that spark of God. Sometimes we don't. Lots of atheists, after all, write stories and screenplays and design video games too, which can be just as good and effective as anything Christians create. But just because they don't see God in their work doesn't mean he isn't there. God doesn't need their permission to speak. He has used and worked through lots of nonbelievers over the years. I don't see why this age of ours should be any different.

God is all around us. And we'll see him if we look.

Not that we should look *everywhere*, mind you.

THE DEVIL: MIND IF I HORN IN?

I have an old Christian pamphlet at my desk titled "This Movie Menace!" in which the author insists that the only good film is an unwatched film. Writes author Holland B. London,

> If you were asked the question, What is public enemy number 1? What would you say? Some would say the Liquor Traffic, others would name the modern dance, others would name the cigarette habit, others would name gambling. There is no question but [t]hat these things that I have mentioned have polluted and distorted our age, but in my opinion the modern movie could well be classified as Public Enemy Number 1. It is positively immoral and rotten. It defies reform, destroys standards of right living and depletes the mind.

The pamphlet, as near as I can figure, was written in the 1940s—a time when something called the Hays Code forbid in movies any overt references to sex, almost any sort of swearing, and if someone was going to mention God, it had to be in the most wholesomely reverential way.

Makes me wonder what Mr. London would think of, say, *The Wolf of Wall Street*.

But the guy has a point. I work for a ministry (*Plugged In*) built around the idea that entertainment can be deeply—and often detrimentally—influential. Studies suggest that problematic content, whether it's sex or violence or just plain worldview issues, can have an impact upon how we think about sex, violence, and the world. As Paul wrote to the Corinthians, "'I have the right to do anything,' you say—but not everything is beneficial. 'I have the right to do anything'—but not everything is constructive" (1 Cor. 10:23 NIV). Entertainment, I think, fits into that dynamic. We have to understand our own strengths and weaknesses. We have to know how seeing or listening to something not only might impact us but also influence those around us. For example, don't take whatever I say in the chapters that will follow as carte blanche to watch, say, *The Walking Dead*.

We've already talked about how God is the ultimate Creator, and how creation is an expression of both his nature and his deep, endless love. Evil doesn't have that ability. If it did, Satan probably would've crafted his own alternate universe and gotten, quite literally, the hell outta here. This means that every aspect of God's creation has a part of God's perfect design in it—including our stories.

But while evil can't create as God can, it can be quite creative in how it twists what God has made. According to Augustine, it's not something as much as it's a corruptive nothing, if that makes sense. If an apple represents God's goodness, evil's the rot that eats at it. If a road is God's goodness, evil's the pothole that ruins your suspension. All evil and sin are, really, corruptions of God's gift to us. Food is great until it turns into gluttony. Working hard is awesome unless it leads to pride or ulcers. Sex is great until it leads to lust and infidelity and porn and who knows what else.

And, wouldn't you know it, everything on earth—*everything*—has in some way been twisted and tainted by evil. If Satan can't make his own universe, well, he'll just do his best (or worst) to fiddle with this one to meet his own needs. And because he's a persistent cuss, there's not one bit of this place, not one person, that doesn't carry a whiff of his persistent, sulfuric odor. Not you, not me, not the street preacher on the corner, not the pope. And naturally, that extends to our own piddly works of creation too. Even the greatest works of spiritual art can't reflect God's beauty perfectly. Even the most beautiful hymns and worship songs can't fully convey the wonder of heaven. Everything's just a little messed up.

Nothing here on earth, except for Jesus himself, is ever purely good. And nothing is ever completely bad, not even *Family Guy*. But while God can work through all possible avenues, that doesn't mean we should use that as an excuse to walk down them all. There is entertainment that can hurt us far more than it can help us, I believe. And the level of hurt can vary depending upon our own weaknesses and sensitivities and life experiences. Don't watch or listen to stuff you're not comfortable with. And even if you are comfortable with it, give your entertainment choices some serious thought.

But even if and when you stumble into a dark place media-wise, God still can be found. The bush can still burn.

DETECTING THE TRUTH

In early 2014, HBO aired its first season of *True Detective*, starring Matthew McConaughey and Woody Harrelson. The show followed detectives Rustin "Rust" Cohle (McConaughey) and

Marty Hart (Harrelson) as they tried to solve a horrific series of murders over the course of seventeen years.

It was extraordinarily graphic; HBO, being a premium television network, practically requires it. Viewers saw sexual encounters, mutilated corpses, and people abused in horrific ways. But it wasn't just the content that was problematic: from its pedophilic pastors to its legion of shadowy demon-worshipers, the program gave viewers a picture of the worst of humankind, and its core philosophy was correspondingly bleak. The dead were unmourned and barely noticed. The living often were little more than beasts, full of lust and anger and horrific predilections that, as they were sated, the camera was more than willing to follow and film.

Rust, a deeply troubled, tortured detective, believed that life was a dark joke that, in the end, led to more darkness. We were "sentient meat," he declared, living in an indifferent, cold universe. The case becomes, for Rust, simply unfinished business—a book he must close before he checks out for good. He'd be the last person you'd expect to be a spiritual conduit.

But when Rust is critically injured in the final episode of season 1, blood gushing out of his gut, he faces the darkness and finds something more.

"I could feel my definitions fading," he tells Marty. "And beneath that darkness there was another kind—it was deeper— warm, like a substance. I could feel—man, I knew, I *knew* my daughter waited for me, there."

Rust goes on with his near-religious epiphany—one that ticked off some atheists who had watched the show and found in Rust one of their own.

"It's just one story," Rust says. "The oldest. Light versus dark."

"Well, I know we ain't in Alaska, but it appears to me that the dark has a lot more territory," a grim Marty answers—a profound, and even biblical, reflection of a fallen world.

"You're looking at it wrong," Rust answers. "Once there was only dark. You ask me, the light's winning."

It's telling that the episode's title was "Form and Void," from Genesis 1:2 (ESV): "The earth was without form and void, and darkness was over the face of the deep. And the Spirit of God was hovering over the face of the waters."

Once there was only dark, Rust says. But we know what comes just one verse later: let there be light.

This fallen world of ours is filled with a lot of problems, most of our own creation. God gave us free will, and we've used that will to mess things up plenty. Our stories—our movies and television shows, our games and music—are no exception. They're fallen too.

But just as God spoke into the formless void, into the darkness in the face of the deep, he speaks into our darkest places too.

Let there be light, he says. And so there is.

CHAPTER 2
FLYING HIGH

Superheroes, God's Call, and the Good Worth Fighting For

I have been shown the path. I must follow where it leads. Like Parsifal, I must confront the unreason that threatens me. I must go alone into the Dark Tower . . . and face the dragon within.
—*Batman: Arkham Asylum* graphic novel

What if **Superman didn't** *want* to be a hero?

He didn't have to be, you know. He could've been a doctor (and saved ever so much money on X-ray machines) or a welder (that heat vision sure comes in handy) or the best FedEx delivery guy ever. He might've been a fantastically fearsome nightclub bouncer or a reality TV star. If he got into sports, he could've lived quite comfortably off the bullion from his gold medals.

Parents tell their kids that they can be anything they want to be. That's a load of dryer lint, of course. Parents lie a lot—especially about what their kids can or cannot realistically do. Except for Jonathan and Martha Kent. When they told their little boy, Clark, that he could do *anything* (perhaps as Clark bench-pressed the family dairy cow), they meant it.

And practically any career he picked would've been far more lucrative than being a superhero (work week: 168 hours, give or take; starting salary: nothing, plus tips). He might've had enough cash to buy a nice little split-level in the Metropolis suburbs—or, at the very least, heat the Fortress of Solitude a little better. (And don't talk to me about Clark's twice-monthly paycheck from the *Daily Planet*. I've been a reporter. I could've made more money donating plasma.)

And yet he chose a life filled with danger, destruction, and frequent contact with deadly kryptonite. He chose to put his (admittedly rugged) life on the line for the good of us all—even though we never even promised him a plate of nachos in the deal. What would possess a guy to use his skills and gifts so thoughtfully, when he could be making gobs of money in Las Vegas?

It's simple: he's been *called* to do so. And I believe that calling, whether it takes the form of eerie ramblings from his dead father or his own Kansas-grown conscience or some sort of quirk of the guy's Kryptonian DNA, originates from another, greater source.

I believe that almost all superheroes are called to their work. They'd have to be, wouldn't they? After all, even us normal folks without heat vision are called by God to take part in his great story—whether we are doctors or bouncers or reality television stars or even writers. We're all part of a plan. Whether we choose to participate or not is up to us. Superheroes are, like we are, asked to follow a higher purpose—to sacrifice something of ourselves for others. If we follow a calling, we're *heroes* (even if our superpowers are kinda lame).

Because heroism isn't about travel-sized grappling hooks hanging on our utility belts. It's about pursuing a higher purpose—following God's will for us, no matter how hard that calling might be. Just like the men and women who wear multicolored spandex for a living. And no, I'm not talking about Zumba instructors.

BORN FOR GREATNESS

Sometimes our heroic callings are pretty obvious early on. For some superheroes, God already seems to have something in mind for them when they're still in their super-absorbent diapers.

From the very beginning of his life, Superman—known then as Kal-El—was clearly special. In 2013's *Man of Steel*, we learn that he was the first naturally born child to come along in centuries. He further separated himself from the rest of Krypton— quite literally, in fact—when his parents packed him away into a tiny spaceship and jettisoned the lad into outer space, thus making him one of the planet's few survivors. (It was especially remarkable he survived, considering he didn't even bring along an extra bottle. Clearly, Kal-El was one remarkable baby.)

Jor-El, Kal-El's natural father, knew his son was going to be something else on earth—both man and god, as it were. "You will give the people an ideal to strive towards," he tells the lad. "They will race behind you, they will stumble, they will fall. But in time, they will join you in the sun." And the very fact that little Kal-El landed where he did—on a small farm in the middle of Kansas, where even a visiting extraterrestrial might learn good Midwestern values and receive a hearty moral upbringing—smacks of destiny too. Would Superman have become Superman had his astro-pod settled down at, say, the Pentagon? Pyongyang? The set of CBS's *Big Brother*? It'd practically take a leap of faith *not* to see a divine hand in Superman's origins.

Jonathan Kent is the first to believe. When he sees Kal-El in his cornfield, he's seeing more than a baby: he sees something greater at work.

"You're the answer, son," he tells him in *Man of Steel*. "You're the answer to, 'Are we alone in the universe?' . . . And I have to believe that you were . . . that you were sent here for a reason, Clark. And even if it takes you the rest of your life, you owe it to yourself to find out what that reason is."

Those are some pretty serious expectations to shoulder from the get-go. Even his outfit is loaded with prophetic foreshadowing, almost as if it were stitched together by the prophet Isaiah. In *Man of Steel*, we learn that the *S* on the chest doesn't stand for *Superman*, as about eight decades' worth of comics might've suggested. Turns out, it's the El family crest—and it means "hope."

GIVEN GIFTS FOR A PURPOSE

Superman's sense of purpose is not that unusual—at least, not in places where costumed crimefighters hang out. So many superheroes carry a sense of destiny that they likely have a special pocket for it—right next to their Batarangs or their extra Cyclops visor.

Sure, not everyone felt that calling from the very beginning like Supes did. The abilities of Marvel's X-Men don't really make their first appearance until adolescence. While other kids were getting pimples and sprouting hair from strange places, mutants start growing wings or shapeshifting or reading minds. *Awwwkwaaard!*

At other times, superheroes acquire their unique abilities not through the miracle of adolescence, but through emotional trauma or huge doses of radiation. Peter Parker never asked to have been bitten by that radioactive spider. The Fantastic Four were just fine being the Ordinary Four before their spaceship flew through that strange radioactive field. Hal Jordan was (mostly) just minding his own business when a dying alien gave him that power ring, granting him the extraordinary powers of the Green Lantern.

And then there are the heroes that don't have special gifts at all. Batman's Bruce Wayne doesn't have any special powers other than his own gumption and bottomless bank account. Tony Stark is a self-made superhero too, crafting several nifty suits of high-tech armor using nothing more than his considerable noggin.

But most superheroes believe that they have a higher calling to follow—a purpose to fulfill. And while that might not sound so spiritual on the surface (atheists talk about their "purpose" and "calling" too), the very language makes some really profound assumptions about both humanity and divinity. To say we are following a calling suggests that something or someone is *calling us* to do something. To say *we* have a purpose presupposes a universe where most *everything* has a purpose—not a universe, in other words, created by chance. Purpose requires design. A calling requires a caller.

This is not to suggest that superheroes are all regular churchgoers. Some express deep spiritual skepticism. But their language and their actions suggest, whether they know it or not, that they buy in to the concept of a higher power—and more important, a moral power, one that expects them to use their gifts and abilities for the benefit of others.

If they didn't make those core assumptions, wouldn't it be natural for these supernaturally gifted people to flake out or find less stressful ways to make a living?

"I shouldn't be alive . . . unless it was for a reason," Tony Stark— admittedly not the most pious of superheroes—tells Pepper Potts in the first *Iron Man* movie. "I'm not crazy, Pepper. I just finally know what I have to do. And I know in my heart that it's right." Professor Charles Xavier, the wheelchair-assisted leader of the X-Men, tells his charges that their abilities are "gifts"—which, intentionally or not, suggests that there must be a giver. In *Spider-Man*, Peter Parker's Uncle Ben tells us that "with great power comes great responsibility," a reminder that nifty powers require a set of moral do's and don'ts to operate correctly. Hal Jordan of the Green Lantern Corps believes that the ring "chose" him, much as God might choose one of us.

Sure, for much of the movie *Green Lantern*, Hal thinks the ring made a big mistake: "The one thing that a Green Lantern is supposed to be is fearless," he whines. "'Fearless' is the job description. That isn't me." But if you check out the Old Testament, you'll find it loaded with a bunch of whiny prophets and servants who thought God made a mistake with them too. Pretty much everyone truly *chosen* for big things believes that God has thrown them into the deep end of the pool with nary a set of water wings. Those so thrown think God must be nuts: that, for the first time in history, the Big Guy's made a mistake. Turns out, the only mistake is made by the ones who are called—underestimating their own gifts, talents, and character that God gave them.

All these superheroes echo a spiritual dynamic at play for all of us: God has plans for us. Dreams. Ambitions. He wants us to do awesome things for him in this world, and he's given us the tools to do so. Sure, not all of us are gifted with superhuman strength or the ability to use our hands as hot plates. Our gifts may be more along the lines of an efficient mind or a dandy singing voice or a beautiful laugh. Sometimes, we uncover or develop gifts later in life. Paul even talks about how we're given "spiritual gifts" along the way (a concept that honestly confuses me a little and carries a wide variety of interpretations).

And sometimes, we experience something in our lives that sets us on a path that we never imagined we'd follow. A health crisis might make you more prone to serving at a hospice. An encounter with a homeless man might turn you into a regular soup kitchen volunteer. I know people who, just through a "chance" encounter, suddenly were convinced they needed to quit their jobs and start ministries to help, say, young women in Africa or orphans in Russia. Some of them are much poorer than they used to be, but they smile a lot more. They say they've found their "calling."

But just because God calls us to do something doesn't mean we have to follow. None of us is just an action figure, to be manipulated at will—not even superheroes (though they often do have their own action figures as well). No, God may be calling us, but he also gives us a choice. And that's reflected in our cinematic superheroes too.

ASKED TO CHOOSE

"One day . . . you're gonna have to make a choice," Jonathan Kent tells his young adopted son, Clark. "You just have to decide what kind of a man you want to grow up to be, Clark; because whoever that man is, good character or bad . . . he's gonna change the world."

In *Man of Steel*, Clark Kent faces that choice when he is thirty-three years old (about the same age most scholars think Jesus was when he was crucified). For most of his life, Clark had kept his real nature hidden from the rest of the world. His adoptive father, Jonathan, thought Clark likely would be rejected if people knew what he really was. And no one, not even a superpowerful Kryptonian, likes rejection.

But then one day, General Zod and some other Kryptonian ne'er-do-wells land on earth and announce to the world's earthlings that there's an extraterrestrial living among them. Zod demands that the people of earth turn the guy in—assuming, of course, that they value their miserable little planet.

Clark doesn't really know what to do. If he turns himself in to Zod, his sacrifice might save the world. Or Zod could break his promise and destroy the place anyway.

So Clark does what any good farm-raised Midwestern Christ-figure might do: he goes to church, pondering his choice as a stained-glass Jesus looks over his shoulder. Eventually a priest comes in, and Clark makes a quick confession, asking for a little advice on what he should do. Can he trust Zod? Or even his fellow humans, for that matter?

"Sometimes," the priest says, "you have to take a leap of faith first. The trust part comes later."

Clark decides to turn himself in. He allows his captors to slap a set of handcuffs on him, and they haul him into custody—crazy, really, since those handcuffs would have all the restraining power of shaving cream. His captors have no real power over him, making the scene an echo of Jesus' own surrender to the authorities of his day.

It's telling that that's the first time we see him dressed as Superman, complete with cape and blue leggings and the big sign of hope across his chest. The suit is both a snappy fashion statement (hey, if it's his last act, he might as well look his Kryptonian best, right?) and a statement of choice: his choice to be a hero. He's taken on the mantle of his own superhumanness and all the responsibilities that entails, even if it means his death.

The fact that he *can* choose is emphasized from the very beginning of *Man of Steel*. His home planet of Krypton was almost completely populated by folks who literally were born and bred to do specific jobs: Jor-El was made to be a scientist; Zod was designed as a soldier. They were given more than a calling; they were given *orders*. And everything in their being required that they follow. But Kal-El, he was different. As the first naturally born child on the planet in centuries, he is, as Jor-El says, "free to forge his own destiny."

See, you need more than superpowers to become a superhero. When you look at characters like Batman, superpowers hardly seem necessary. Sure, extraordinary abilities make our superheroes *super*, but it's their *choices* that make the *hero*. Each caped wonder in our Technicolor pantheon makes choices to follow the right path or the wrong one. Each choice defines who he or she is. And if a would-be superhero should choose poorly? Then he or she joins a fraternity of an altogether different sort.

Take a look at our X-Men friend, Professor Charles Xavier, and his one-time BFF Erik Lehnsherr, aka Magneto. Both are really powerful mutants: Professor X can, among other things, read and even manipulate peoples' minds, and Magneto can telekinetically play with all sorts of metal. Both keenly feel the prejudice of the nonmutant people around them. And both, as we saw in *X-Men: First Class*, started out on the same team. And sometimes, as happened in *X-Men: Days of Future Past*, they join forces again.

But for the most part, they made different choices. Xavier and the mutants under his tutelage opted to work within the confines of law and with humanity to encourage acceptance—battling evildoers whenever appropriate. Magneto became an evildoer (though he might classify himself as a freedom fighter), declaring war on humanity and rallying legions of mutants to his own nefarious banner. Almost every mutant, it would seem, falls under sway of one of these two leaders. Each mutant makes a choice to become a hero or a villain.

"When an individual acquires great power, the use or misuse of that power is everything," Professor Xavier says in *X-Men: The Last Stand*. "Will it be used for the greater good? Or will it be used for personal or for destructive ends? Now this is a question we must all ask ourselves. Why? Because we are mutants."

Xavier tells his students—and us—that being good isn't a matter of fate: it's a matter of choice.

Perhaps the ultimate illustration of this power of choice and free will is the weird and ruddy superhero Hellboy.

In the 2004 movie *Hellboy*, we learn that he came to earth via interdimensional portal—the cutest little demon with the Right Hand of Doom you ever did see. But a young scientist named Trevor Bruttenholm, refusing to judge a baby by its horns, adopted the creature and raised him as a Catholic. And in the movies—so far, at least—the rosary-toting demon (Red, for short) has taken his father's teachings to heart and tries to do the right thing. Never mind the diabolical prophecy that claims he'll bring about the end of the world; it seems as though Red's own decisions are trumping his diabolical "destiny."

It's a powerful message: God's grace is so powerful that it can rescue *anyone*—even a horned demon—who wants to follow him.

We don't know how all this will work out in the movies, if it works out at all. Audiences were left hanging at the end of *Hellboy II*, and *Hellboy III* seems an uncertain enterprise. But for now, the trajectory is encouraging: Red shows us that we can *all* choose what sorts of people we want to be. No matter what sort of baggage we carry, no matter how troubled our past has been, our life is not written in stone. We can choose to be one of the good guys. We've got free will in our corner. And if we *choose* to embrace the saving mercy of Jesus, none of us is beyond his mercy.

FIGHTING FOR TRUTH, JUSTICE, AND ALL THAT STUFF

We've seen that superheroes, like us, are called for great things. We know that they, and we, must choose to follow that call. But there's one other trait of superhero-dom that is worth mentioning here—and that's what these demigods are, in fact, choosing.

Again, most superheroes won't come right out and say that they're explicitly Christian warriors, following God's call like legions of particularly muscular Billy Grahams. I do not expect to see Professor Xavier sharing the gospel with Magneto over a chess game. I doubt that Superman would invite Lois Lane to a Switchfoot concert. This is a secular age, and even the most religiously zealous superhero would be culturally sensitive. And many superheroes may not know exactly what calling they're following.

A few years ago, I wrote a book that dealt with finding spirituality in the Batman mythos. Some folks thought that was just plain crazy, given that Batman sometimes (depending on what comic you read) talks an awful lot like an agnostic or an atheist. And really, his life experience almost could be seen as a litany of difficult-to-answer theological questions. For example, how could a loving God have allowed Batman's parents to die? How could a caring God tolerate the societal abyss that is Gotham City?

Batman *has* prayed, of course. It was, in fact, during a prayer that he committed his life to fighting crime. But if we say, just for the sake of argument, that Batman *is* an atheist, he's really terrible at it.

Atheism, by definition, doesn't allow for the existence of God. And without God—or, at least, some sort of karmic force in the universe—it seems like morality is a trickier thing to pin down.

This is not to say that atheists are immoral. Far from it. I've known many atheists who were way more moral than some Christians I could mention. But in the mind of an atheist, morality would seem to be, by necessity, a man-made creation, and as such it'd be a little squishier. Notions of true "good" and true "evil" would be inherently more relative: without a definitive source to tell us what "good" is, we're left to make it up for ourselves, and so good becomes whatever we say it is—whether it's helpful or beneficial to our communities and whatnot. For someone who truly buys into the concept of a godless universe, there wouldn't be anything inherently, cosmically "bad" about murder, for instance; it's bad because we say it is. And as such, atheists are way more reluctant than we judgmental Christians to force their notions of what "good" is on other people.

Batman, though, is not one for relativity. He believes that killing is wrong—no matter what. He believes that evildoers must be punished. Granted, he's not big on following Gotham's posted speed limits, and he certainly wouldn't be prone to obeying a citywide curfew. But even that further illustrates the point: right and wrong does not come from humanity, Batman believes, but elsewhere. He doesn't follow Gotham's rules to the letter because he adheres to and follows a higher set of laws, immutable by any person or earthbound power. He believes in a right and wrong that surpasses both human jurisdiction and human understanding.

That trait is embraced by every superhero I know of: the idea that there is good and evil in the world, that there are rights and wrongs. These superpowered men and women may be able to heave cars over buildings or fry eggs with their eyes, but for all their power they humble themselves to this even more powerful truth. They choose to submit to a higher calling, a higher rule. And in the end, they'd be willing to die for it.

Superheroes practically fall all over themselves to sacrifice for a better purpose. We see it in almost every Marvel- or DC-universe movie out there. Most often and most obviously, it's with their lives. In 2011's *Captain America: The First Avenger,* Cap pilots an airplane of doom carrying a weapon of unimaginable destruction into freezing Arctic waters, going down with his airship. In 2014's *Captain America: The Winter Soldier,* a resurrected Cap does it *again*—putting down his fists and laying down his life for the very soul of his old, and now corrupted, friend, Bucky. A temporarily human Thor (in the 2011 film of the same name) matches himself against an extraterrestrial robot to save the residents of a small New Mexico town, even though he knows it will be his death. Even Tony Stark, the silver screen's most selfish superhero, nearly dies in 2012's *The Avengers* by flying through a wormhole with a nuclear weapon to save earth.

All in a day's work for the costumed crimefighter, of course: when it's your job to protect the world from four-hundred-foot-tall robots or interdimensional spiders or diabolical fire-breathing houseplants, you know that some life-risking derring-do is just part of the job description.

Most of us probably never will be asked to die for anything. But we are called to submit to a higher authority—and through our submission, that means we might be asked to make some sacrifices for the greater good along the way. These sacrifices are, by definition, never easy. We are selfish creatures.

But we are led to be better than that. We're asked to transcend our own weaknesses and frailty, just as the superheroes we see in the movies and read about in the comics are. We are called. And when it comes right down to it, our calling isn't much different than the one Superman himself received. We are asked to serve our fellow human and the One who made us. And we don't even have to fly to do it.

CHAPTER 3

IT'S THE END OF THE WORLD (AS WE KNOW IT)

Dystopian Movies and the Secret Hope Left
After All the Canned Goods Are Gone

Interviewer: Can you destroy the earth?
The Tick: Egad, I hope not! That's where I keep all my stuff!
—*The Tick: The Animated Series,* season 1, episode 7
("The Tick vs. the Tick")

U nless it involves sleeping in, the end of the world is pretty much guaranteed to suck.

That's what our movies tell us, anyway. And science too. Go ahead—just try to think of a cheery apocalyptic scenario. I dare you. And no cheating by bringing the Rapture into it. Would the end be any peppier if brought about by, say, characters from My Little Pony? If we keeled over from a pestilence of uncontrollable laughter? If we were all buried in bacon raining down from the heavens, would the apocalypse seem more (*ahem*) savory? No, I tell you. Once we'd all eaten twenty or thirty pounds of the stuff, even the thickest, crispiest bacon would seem hateful to us. We'd lament how it was making our hair and hipster beards all greasy, how sickening its crackle sounded underneath our feet, how difficult it was to dress well when our underwear drawers were forever filling with Canadian bacon. We'd cry and pray, beseeching God to remove this hateful deluge of pork products—to spare our world from the hovering Piggy of Death.

No, the End, whatever form it takes (again, barring any Rapturing), is bound to be unpleasant. And thanks to the entertainment industry, we can imagine dozens, nay, *hundreds* of ways the End might come. Because if there's one thing that Hollywood likes to do, it's to destroy everything we know and charge us twelve bucks to watch.

And then, of course, movies and television dare us to ponder the ultimate oxymoron: What will people do *after* the End—what sort of world will they find when they crawl outside their bacon fallout shelters and survey the salty, and probably stinky, world left behind? These dystopian fantasies imagine civilization's remnants slowly, painfully trying to deal with past destruction and looking toward a future that doesn't involve eating their neighbor's dog—or in a pinch, their neighbor.

Lately the entertainment industry has treated us to maybe hundreds of end-of-the-world-and-after stories, and all of them either show, or assume, the death of millions or even billions of people. In the movie *2012* (released, oddly enough, in 2009), director Roland Emmerich might've killed off around 7.2 billion people via earthquakes, volcanoes, storms, and floods, leaving just a tiny remnant left to rebuild. Rarely has such annihilation been seen onscreen in such detail. (And it's been called a family film. Go figure.)

But even in the midst of these truly doomsday scenarios, we still can hear some prophetic voices of light and hope in the darkness. And I guess that makes sense, given that prophets were always at their noisy best in a crisis.

IT WAS THE BEST OF TIMES
IN THE WORST OF TIMES

Things don't get much worse than in Emmerich's *2012*. Set in a world where the earth's core is rapidly overheating and our magnetic poles are about to go Miley Cyrus levels of crazy, our heroes had to dodge lava flows, leap gaping chasms, and swim through flooding arks to even have a *chance* to make it to the movie's credits. Stress? Anxiety? Yeah, your geometry test or work presentation doesn't have a thing on these kinds of apocalyptic ulcers. The first thing grocery stores likely ran out of was Pepto-Bismol. "Kind of galling when you realize that nutbags with cardboard signs had it right the whole time," says Carl Anheuser, the movie's slimy White House chief of staff.

Most of us aren't exactly pictures of serenity under stress. We tend to get snippy. We say and do things that later we feel ashamed of. When my basement flooded in a rainstorm, did I turn to my wife and quip, "Well, at least we have that indoor pool we always wanted"? No. I sat on the basement stairs and fumed at the unfairness of it all. Never mind that there are people who've lost so much more in floods or that people have died in them. I just kept thinking, "God, how could you do this to me?! We just put in new carpet!" Part of me wanted to just leave and never return, 'cause that's how I sometimes deal with stress. (Avoidance is a popular but expensive coping skill.)

The floods were a little worse in *2012*, and we'd expect people to be correspondingly more nasty. And some, in fact, are. Carl Anheuser isn't exactly a picture of grace under pressure. He knows of a small, supersecret fleet of "arks" that were built to rescue the best, brightest, and richest people on the planet. And he does his utmost to keep the truth—both of doomsday and of the existence of these massive lifeboats—from everyone as long as possible, sometimes even killing those who nearly let the secret slip.

"What did you think?" he asks heroic geologist Adrian Helmsley. "We're all just gonna get onboard, hold hands and sing 'Kumbaya'?"

But in the face of the very end of the world, many characters reveal a better character. They take stock of what's really important to them—and for our heroes, that comes down to the stuff the Bible tells us is important: family; friends; God; doing the right thing. We see characters risk their lives for near strangers or spend their final minutes with the people who matter most to them. "The moment we stop fighting for each other, that's the moment we lose our humanity," Adrian says.

Thomas Wilson, president of the United States, gives up his place on an ark. He spends some time praying ("Under these circumstances that's not such a bad idea," Carl is told), then addresses the world via a waning video feed. "Today, none of us are strangers," he says. "Today, we are one family, stepping into the darkness together." And the president closes his remarks by beginning to recite Psalm 23 . . . before the end hits.

Despite all the destruction, *2012* is buoyed with a quiet dignity and contagious optimism. When the world is at its worst, humanity has a choice: to fall in step with the cold, anxiety-riddled pragmatism of Carl; or to respond as Adrian and President Wilson do, by pushing and fighting and cherishing what we love as long as hope remains; and should that hope be removed, to always remember that come what may, we are in God's hands.

Both of the latter are biblical responses to stress. Consider what the prophet Isaiah wrote in his book (chap. 40, vv. 30-31):

> *Youths will become tired and weary,*
> *young men will certainly stumble;*
> > *but they who hope in the LORD*
> *will renew their strength;*
> *they will fly up on wings like eagles;*
> *they will run and not be tired;*
> *they will walk and not be weary.*

And then there's this from John 14:27: "Peace I leave with you. My peace I give to you. I give to you not as the world gives. Don't be troubled or afraid."

Keep in mind, these passages were written in moments when readers would've been living out some dystopian dramas of their own, and they thought their *own* worlds were coming to an end. Isaiah lived when the Assyrians were collecting kingdoms like signed baseballs and killing off most of the previous owners. John was encouraging shiny new Christians not to give up the faith— never mind that believers might wind up a tasty midafternoon meal for a Colosseum lion. The Bible encourages us to display grace under the most extreme sorts of pressure. And that extends even to displaying sacrificial grace when there's a greater good at hand.

GIVING YOUR ALL—LITERALLY

When it comes to sacrificial stories, few can top *The Hunger Games* trilogy.

If you're familiar with the story at all, you know that the Games themselves are all about a different kind of sacrifice—more in the mold of an Old Testament, *let's-kill-this-kid-to-appease-Moloch* sort of way. Decades ago, we learn, there was a huge civil war in the land of Panem (which, if you look at a map of the place, looks suspiciously like the United States), leaving the country severely underpopulated and woefully depressed. The victors in Panem's Capitol, in an effort both to punish the rebels and to cheer themselves up (though it certainly doesn't help their population issues), decide to launch the Hunger Games—a televised killfest that's part *Gladiator*, part *Survivor*. Each of Panem's twelve districts is required to ship off two youngsters (one male, one female) to participate. Only one of those twenty-four contestants is supposed to walk out of the arena alive. (The ancient Aztecs would've been so proud.)

The Hunger Games is the worst reality show ever. The citizens of Panem need this sort of fame like they need a hole in their heads. (And alas, sometimes they get both.) But when twelve-year-old Primrose Everdeen gets selected as District 12's tribute for the Hunger Games, her big sister, Katniss, does something dramatic. "With one sweep of my arm, I push her behind me," she says in Suzanne Collins's *The Hunger Games* book. "'I volunteer!' I gasp. 'I volunteer as tribute!'"

This moment, in both the book and the movie, is a burning bush-like echo. The gesture carries with it a hint of an even greater sacrifice made in Jerusalem two thousand years ago, when someone hung on a cross that was meant for us. And it's just the first of many such sacrifices we see as the series barrels on with ruthless momentum.

Peeta Mellark, selected alongside Katniss, is determined to help Kat win the thing—even though he knows it'll mean he will die. And then when *both* inexplicably walk out of the arena (much to the Capitol's chagrin) and *both* are sent to the next Hunger Games (much to the Capitol's cackling glee)—a sort of All-Star edition of the show—each is determined to die for the other. They fight about who's going to give up whose life for whom, so that it begins to look like a really demented argument for a dinner check. (*"I'll* die for *you* this time. I insist." "No, Peeta. It's *my* turn. Give me the berries.")

But it never comes to that, what with all the tributes giving up their lives for *both* Katniss and Peeta, who've become symbols for a greater, more-rebellious movement to overthrow the Capitol. Sacrifice in *The Hunger Games: Catching Fire,* the second part of the trilogy, is all the rage. One elderly tribute, Mags, dives into a poisonous fog, allowing Katniss and her allies to save themselves. Another tribute dies by evil monkey—leaping in front of Peeta to save him from the primate's nasty teeth. Turns out, several tributes weren't in it to win it: they were determined to help Katniss and Peeta survive.

The first two *Hunger Games* books and movies reverberate with echoes of ancient Rome. The city sat at the administrative and economic heart of a far-flung empire made of disparate and subjugated people, separated into provinces. It was said that all roads led there, and all the empire's wealth flowed into the capital, creating a wondrous city of excess and debauchery. Rome's leaders figured that the city's population could be kept in line through distraction, and thus sponsored wild and bloody games, most notably in the Colosseum. (The phrase associated with these grotesque festivals, "bread and circuses," reads in Latin, *panem et circenses*. Coincidence? Hardly. The final book even references the quote.)

No one really knows how many Christians died in these "games"—which often amounted to ornate and grotesque public executions. We know that Rome blamed Christians for the empire's problems (much as the Capitol blamed Katniss and company for their woes) and wasn't shy about killing them. About twenty thousand Christians are said to have died during the reign of the Roman Emperor Diocletian alone.

But as in *The Hunger Games* movies, the persecution itself becomes a key contributor to the growth of Christianity and, ultimately, the Christianization of the Roman Empire itself. We're told that many of these Christian martyrs faced death with serenity, willing to sacrifice their lives for a greater good—the hope that Christianity offered. "I am as the grain of the field and must be ground by the teeth of the lions, that I may become fit for [God's] table," Ignatius reportedly said before he had the dubious honor of being the first Christian to be executed by lion in the Colosseum. Had it been me, my last words would've been more like, "Aaaaaauuugghhhh!"

For Christians in ancient Rome, every day must've felt like the end of the world. Honestly, they probably felt a lot like the folks in Panem did. Life was pretty horrible for most, and liable to be pretty short for many. It's easy to lose hope in times like those. And yet, as we see in lots of dystopian stories, hope is often the only thing people have left.

A CATALYST FOR HOPE

"For practical purposes," G. K. Chesterton wrote in his book *Heretics*, "it is at the hopeless moment that we require the hopeful man, and the virtue either does not exist at all, or begins to exist at that moment. Exactly at the instant when hope ceases to be reasonable it begins to be useful."

Our movies—particularly our most desperately perilous movies—prove it. In movies that show the world at its worst and most grotesque, you'll often see a surprising thread of hope. In *The Road Warrior*, Mad Max (Mel Gibson) is surprisingly willing to sacrifice himself to help a tiny pocket of civilization find safety and new hope. In Tom Cruise's 2013 flick *Oblivion*, a mechanic turns on a mechanized mothership to help protect the scraps of humanity left on earth, offering hope for better days ahead. Even in 1927's *Metropolis*—the silent granddaddy of all dystopian flicks and a film all movie junkies probably should see—you will find hope in the midst of revolution.

The world of *Metropolis* bears a certain resemblance to Panem, a land in which the haves and the have-nots live in separate worlds, except in *Metropolis*, the have-nots rarely even get to see the sun.

The rich live in a spectacularly luxurious city above ground. The poor live deep under the earth, their only job to feed and care for monstrous machines.

A woman named Maria keeps the workers' spirits up, literally preaching (in front of candles and crosses and everything) a combination of grace and justice and hope for a better life in the future. So how do you solve a problem like Maria? Through technology, of course! A nasty scientist crafts a metal facsimile of Maria (which stands in front of an inverted pentagram), that masquerades as the real Maria, whips workers into a frenzy, and encourages them to destroy—well, pretty much everything. In their zeal, though, they flood their underground city and nearly kill all of their kids.

It's pretty much a worst-case scenario for Metropolis, and given that this movie is German (Germany, particularly between World Wars I and II, was not a country known for its sunny outlook), you'd half expect Metropolis to be completely gutted by fire and water and a sinister metal Maria. But the real Maria and her well-to-do beau, Freder, risk their lives to save the children, fake Maria is burned at the stake (still laughing demonically), and everyone makes up, solemnly promising to do better. Against all odds, hope lives on—even without color or sound.

SOURCE OF HOPE

Metropolis uses lots of Christian imagery and biblical references to make its point—perhaps not so surprising, given the more pious era in which it was made. Back when *Metropolis* was in theaters, most folks watching believed that God indeed was the source of ultimate hope.

We live in a more secular age now, of course. Faith can feel a little antiquated in some circles, and even the concept of hope itself has been diminished. We hope for a good grade in chemistry. We hope that little Chucky Sue notices us. We hope for better weather tomorrow or an easy drive home or that our boss won't yell at us for being late again. Our hopes seem smaller these days. Pettier. It seems as though few of us really hope for a significantly better world anymore.

If society places its hope in anything, really, it's in the relentless march of science. Science will help us feed the hungry. Science will help us cure the sick. Science will clean up our environment and protect us from outside threats and tuck us safely in at night.

And, hey, I buy in to that to some extent. I like my iPhone, dig my microwave, and love the fact that my dentist doesn't have to get me liquored up to fill a tooth.

But dystopian movies tend to be skeptical of science, seeing it as much a force for evil as for good. *Metropolis* might've been one of the first movies to express a cynicism of science's cure-all powers, but it certainly wasn't the last. You don't need to keep *The Terminator* in your permanent Netflix cue to get the message.

No, in the movies, hope seems to spring from another source, and I think often a spiritual source. And even now, in our more secular age, the flicks we see can make that source surprisingly explicit.

Denzel Washington's *The Book of Eli* (2010) is part Mad Max, part Billy Graham. The world in which Eli lives is a pretty bleak one—a land torn apart by war, littered with the dead and plagued

by cannibals. But Eli carries with him a talisman of great hope—
the world's very last Bible. And he believes he's been tasked with
the sacred duty of protecting the book and ushering it into a safe
place. No matter that the guy's been wandering in this postapoc-
alyptic wilderness for thirty years. Never mind he's completely
blind. As he tells a new traveler, Solara, "I walk by faith, not by
sight." Solara's doubtful, though. Even the concept of faith doesn't
make sense to her.

"It doesn't have to make sense," Eli insists. "It's faith, it's faith.
It's the flower of light in the field of darkness that's giving me the
strength to carry on. You understand?"

"Is that from your book?" Solara asks.

Eli pauses. "No, it's, uh, Johnny Cash, *Live at Folsom Prison.*"

For Eli, faith and hope are bound up in the book that he's
carrying—and the God who gave it to him.

NEW LIFE IN DEATH

In 2006, *Gravity* director Alfonso Cuarón unveiled the R-rated
Children of Men, considered by some to be one of the best movies
of the twenty-first century. The premise: humankind has collec-
tively turned infertile. There hasn't been a baby born in eighteen
years, and civilization is in its death throes. Only in England do
we find a semblance of order, and that's fading quickly. Everyone,
including our hero, Theo (Clive Owen), is pushing through life
without any hope at all.

And then one day, Theo's given the task of safeguarding a young
woman named Kee—one who, we learn, is pregnant.

For two thousand years, the story of God's sudden, outlandish arrival on earth as a little baby has been told and retold, celebrated and recelebrated and gurgitated and regurgitated until the power of the message has almost become meaningless. We set up our Christmas trees and rip open our gifts and sing "Silent Night" with the words barely registering. Sometimes, our most precious stories must be retold in shocking form for us to hear them.

Children of Men is the most shocking nativity story imaginable. In Kee's baby—born in the midst of a furious battle—we are given a window into ancient Bethlehem, when hope itself was wrapped tightly and set inside a manger. In Cuarón's fable—released on Christmas Day in the United States—characters marvel at the creation of being, the renewal of spirit. They react as Christians *should* react to Jesus: *The world need not spin itself to extinction. There is life here. There is light. There is hope.* And it's a hope that Theo is willing, even grateful, to give his life for.

Though Cuarón downplayed or excised some of the Christian themes found in P. D. James's original book, the film retains its inherent spirituality. Even the title echoes Scripture. "Thou turnest man to destruction; and sayest, Return, ye children of men." reads Psalm 90:3 (KJV), a passage that emphasizes God's power and acknowledges the potential for wrath, retribution, and destruction. And yet that very psalm, like the movie, ends with hope:

> *Make us happy for as the same amount of time that you*
>   *afflicted us—*
> *for the same number of years that we saw only trouble.*
> *Let your acts be seen by your servants;*

let your glory be seen by their children.
Let the kindness of the Lord our God be over us.
Make the work of our hands last.
Make the work of our hands last!

A SHINING FUTURE

The end of the world bites. Whether it comes about via fire or aliens or a cataclysmic rise in cholesterol levels, it won't be fun for anyone.

But here's the thing about the end: it precedes a beginning.

We've seen it in every movie we've talked about: *Metropolis, The Hunger Games, Children of Men, 2012* . . . . Disaster was followed by new creation. After the darkness came the sunrise. When it comes to these movies, Scarlett O'Hara was right: tomorrow *is* another day.

Director Darren Aronofsky's *Noah*, released in 2014, was loathed by lots of Christians, and I understand why. The movie significantly deviates from its biblical source material (at least, I've never come across any rock monsters in *my* translation), and if you were thinking I'm going to suggest that you might glean some good things from *Noah*, you might've hurled this book across the room already. So let me pause for a minute to let you retrieve the book or buy a new iPad.

The trick with *Noah* is to, if at all possible, separate it completely from the source material. If we're able to do that, we find that Aronofsky's *Noah* is, oddly enough, pretty redemptive.

The movie is as dystopian as it comes. Noah and his tiny family seem like they're alone in a world full of nasty, destructive people who could've come straight from a Mad Max movie (minus the motorcycles). The world is so weighed down by wickedness that it's a wonder the place has kept spinning for as long as it has. Now, God's ready to push the reset button. The Creator tells Noah (through a pair of visions) that he plans to send a massive flood to wash away humanity's grievous sins. But before he does, Noah has to build a big boat and usher two of every living animal on board.

He's supposed to take a little hope with him too. But Noah leaves that behind.

See, Noah comes to realize that God didn't drown *all* the world's evil. Noah and his family are also flawed beings, prone to temptation and sin and anger, just as we all are. For the fullness of God's new plan to come to fruition, Noah decides that he and his family must die, one way or another.

Yes, Noah was willing to sacrifice mightily for a higher ideal—to give up, literally, everything. But for Noah, that sacrifice would mean sacrificing his own granddaughters . . . and the future of the human race itself. And though his family insists that Noah misunderstood God—that what he's supposedly being asked to do is out of the Lord's character—Noah will not be dissuaded.

Until, that is, his granddaughters are born and Noah comes close to them to do this terrible, world-crushing deed. He can't kill them. He simply can't. He's not rebelling against God, like the rest of humanity had. It's not that he received new directions from on high.

"I looked down at those two little girls," he tells their mother, "and all I had in my heart was love." And in this moment of love, the world finds new hope. A new beginning.

It's a New Testament message set atop this weird retelling of an Old Testament story—an illustration of the power of grace and a hint of God's own divine mercy. See, we, like Noah's grandkids, are deeply flawed and scarred. We inevitably fall away from God's design and mar his creation. We are imperfect, sinful beings, incompatible with God's perfect nature. And if God wanted everything to truly reflect his awesomeness, we'd have to go.

And yet, we're here. We're loved. When God looks down on us—no matter how much we fail, no matter how much we sin—God feels love. He loves us like nothing else can. This is not an act of charity on God's part; it is an act of boundless devotion of him to us. He takes us in his arms and holds us tight, flaws and all.

"The foolishness of God is wiser than human wisdom, and the weakness of God is stronger than human strength," Paul tells us in 1 Corinthians 1:25. It's in his remarkable, unreasonable love for us, it seems to me, where God is at his most foolish. His weakest. He has a weakness for us, and there is nothing in the universe more beautiful.

The world as we know it really will end one day, of course. You don't need to be a Christian to know that. Whether it ends via a battle on the plains of Armageddon or through climate change, through a sudden supernova or our getting overrun by linguistically gifted apes, time will take a turn for the worse.

And yet in each ending, we can find a new beginning. In each disaster we can find hope. Even if our technology tears us down or our anger blows us up or our wisdom and strength fail us, the foolishness of God will still be there with us, loving us. Even when the world stops spinning.

CHAPTER 4

WE'RE GONNA NEED A BIGGER BOOK

Dealing with Monsters—and Learning from Them Too

Follow only if ye be men of valor! For the entrance to this cave is guarded by a creature so foul, so cruel, that no man yet has fought with it and lived! Bones of full fifty men lie strewn about its lair! So! Brave knights! If you do doubt your courage or your strength, come no further, for death awaits you all with nasty, big, pointy teeth . . .

—Tim the Enchanter (John Cleese), *Monty Python and the Holy Grail*

Nothing can spoil a perfectly good day quicker than finding a monster the size of metropolitan Lubbock in your backyard. The petunias are ruined. The swing set is toast. Fido is suspiciously absent, and you imagine the little pellet of metal at the monster's feet was once the family grill—or worse, the family sedan. And the neighbors, once they see what the thing did to the fence, are almost sure to complain.

Monsters are almost impossible to get rid of once they arrive. They're like dandelions in that way, if dandelions had claws and fangs and the Unblinking Nostril of Doom. Few, if any, exterminators specialize in monster eradication, and the National Guard might have better things to do. Getting rid of 'em often falls to us.

Thankfully, we don't have to worry about such things very often. Why, it's been *months* since my last monster infestation, and both my grill and I are quite grateful. But even if we don't find our-selves in the migration path of Japanese *Kaiju* or central European werewolves or unholy creatures of nightmare, we all still have mon-sters to face. They whisper to us in our quiet moments or haunt our dreams. They play on our weaknesses and revel in our fears. They can paralyze us just as efficiently as Dracula's gaze could. They can make us want to scream or cry, or simply curl up into a fetal ball and do nothing at all. Sure, maybe you haven't worried about monsters since the last one abandoned its place under your bed and left for Aruba. But there's plenty to be afraid of out there.

So when it comes to monsters, be they real or metaphorical, how do we deal with them? We don't have nukes to deal with a wandering Godzilla. Our wooden stakes—ideal weapons to fend off vampires—are lost in the garage somewhere. And very often, our *other* monsters, the ones that stalk our jobs or schools or fam-ily lives, seem just as big (and far more frightening) than anything we saw in *Pacific Rim*. How can we, lacking the chain guns and ripped abs of our cinematic heroes and heroines, hope to tackle these beasts?

Ah, but when you watch monster movies closely, you'll find there's more at work than just gadgetry and a pretty face or two.

COLLECTING COURAGE

"Fairy tales do not give the child the idea of the evil or the ugly," G. K. Chesterton wrote in an essay titled "The Red Angel." "That is in the child already, because it is in the world already. . . . The baby has known the dragon intimately ever since he had an imagination. What the fairy tale provides for him is a St. George to kill the dragon."

In the Western world, the dragon has been a symbol for evil and the devil ever since medieval times and perhaps before. And perhaps there's no dragon in moviedom quite as sinister as Smaug in 2013's *The Hobbit: The Desolation of Smaug*. Not the sort of lizard you'd toast marshmallows with.

Just how big a creep is he? A few decades ago (we are told), the dragon swept into Lonely Mountain, killed every dwarf in sight, and took possession of the underground kingdom's massive treasure as if he were Middle-earth's very own Internal Revenue Service. (Not to insinuate the IRS often immolates people; that only happens, according to Form BS-14TE/27B, should an audit go particularly poorly.) And Smaug sure ain't gonna give it up for thirteen scruffy-looking dwarves, no matter what sort of rightful claims they have.

Thorin Oakenshield, rightful king of Lonely Mountain, knows that the dragon (notoriously cranky beasts) will be tricky to deal with. So what does he do? He sends Bilbo Baggins—a meek, breakfast-loving hobbit who once thought (probably) that earwigs were the height of terrifying—to deal with the thing.

And so he does. Bilbo carries on a lengthy conversation with Smaug, exhibiting bravery that his bearded pals don't initially exhibit. 'Course, he had a little help—a little magic ring that he picked up in another mountain range a movie ago. And Bilbo nearly confesses as much.

"You've changed, Bilbo Baggins," Gandalf tells him. "You're not the same hobbit as the one who left the Shire."

"I was going to tell you," Bilbo stammers. "I found something in the goblin tunnels."

"Found what? What did you find?"

Bilbo pauses, then decides to keep his secret weapon secret for just a little while longer.

"My courage," he says.

Bilbo misled Gandalf here, but he didn't lie. Yes, the ring has some pretty nifty powers. Yes, the ring kept Bilbo from getting fricasseed by Smaug. But it didn't lift Bilbo up and carry him into the mountain; Bilbo walked himself. That took guts, magic ring or no. It wasn't the ring that gave Bilbo courage; it was the monsters.

If Bilbo had stayed home and simply found the ring at Bag End, he'd have no real need for courage. (Well, not until the Ringwraiths showed up, anyway.) He might've continued to tend to his garden and eaten his daily second breakfast and never had cause to discover the secret strength that was hiding inside him. But had the reverse been true—had he gone on the adventure and never found the ring—he still would've been asked to show some backbone. And even when he's ringless (as we see with the trolls in *The Hobbit: An Unexpected Journey*), he does just fine. The ring was forged in the fires of Mount Doom, perhaps, but Bilbo's character was hammered and honed by goblins and dragons and spiders. He found his courage, all right. The ring was just an afterthought.

"Courage is not simply one of the virtues, but the form of every virtue at the testing point," C. S. Lewis writes in *The Screwtape Letters*. "A chastity or honesty, or mercy, which yields to danger will be chaste or honest or merciful only on conditions. Pilate was merciful till it became risky."

It could be argued that Bilbo found courage only *because* it became risky. Because, in the presence of monsters, he had no other choice. But that's the thing about monsters: they force us to make a choice, and often a frightening one. When Pilate was faced with a monstrous mob, he quailed. When Bilbo was faced with a monstrous dragon, he stood strong.

In almost every monster movie, what sets apart the heroes from the extras? The direction in which they run. The people we remember are those who virtually slip into their robotic avatars in *Pacific Rim*, who dare stalk Dracula in the London streets, who risk tangling with the fearsome, fire-wheezing Smaug. Everyone else is chaff, blown away by the dragon's breath.

Courage is great. It's absolutely necessary, in fact, when dealing with monsters. But sometimes we show our greatest courage when we stand up and do . . . nothing.

FINDING PATIENCE

In the 2014 version of *Godzilla*, the world is faced with a *big* crisis. Two of them, actually. A couple of prehistoric beasts called M.U.T.O.s (which stands for "Massive Unidentified Terrestrial Organism," never mind that one of them flies) have awoken and are making their way to San Francisco to have monster sex and create a whole bunch of mini-M.U.T.O.s (*M.M.U.T.O.s?*). Clearly, this development is a bad thing for humanity in general and San Franciscans in particular. Why, if their city is destroyed, where will they go for their high-priced lattes? The media are suspiciously silent.

Clearly, something *must* be done.

The Japanese, given their experience with gigantic monsters, get first crack at it. They try to trap one of the M.U.T.O.s in a nuclear power plant before the thing even crawls out of its giant cocoon, hoping to keep it there, I guess, for all eternity. What will they do with it? Who knows. Perhaps they hope to domesticate it and keep it as a pet. But no matter: the plan doesn't work. The M.U.T.O. pulls himself out of the trap, killing lots of people and destroying a good many towers in the process, and lumbers on his way.

Next up, the American military swings into action. They've got tanks, ships, drones, really expensive socket wrenches . . . pretty much everything that might come in handy in case of a monster attack. And if all that fails, they've got nukes! Big ones! Never mind that the M.U.T.O.s actually *eat* nuclear energy . . . they won't be eating so well when all that nuclear energy comes down and *whomps on their strangely insectoid butts*! In your *face*, M.U.T.O.s!

But Dr. Serizawa, the wise Japanese scientist who has been watching the crisis unfold from the beginning, has another idea: Godzilla. He believes that this monstrous creature may be nature's way of restoring balance on earth—an apex predator specially designed to take down these fearsome M.U.T.O.s. "The arrogance of men is thinking nature is in their control and not the other way around," he tells us. Serizawa's solution is to sit back and let the creatures fight.

This passive solution does not come comfortably to us. When faced with a crisis—when dealing with monsters—we have a need to act, even if acting is ineffective or counterproductive. We need to feel like we're in control. We have to do *something*.

But sometimes God tells us that that's exactly what we have to do. God, like Godzilla, is bigger than any monster we might face. And no matter what, we rest in his very capable hands.

> *But those who hope in the* LORD
> *will renew their strength,*

we read in Isaiah 40:31.

> *They will fly up on wings like eagles;*
> *they will run and not be tired;*
> *they will walk and not be weary.*

In Psalm 33:20-22, we read,

> *We put our hope in the* LORD.
> *He is our help and our shield.*
> *Our heart rejoices in God,*
> *because we trust his holy name.*
> LORD, *let your faithful love surround us,*
> *because we wait for you.*

It's not comfortable to wait. It's not very satisfying to trust. The Bible's full of folks who wonder how long God'll keep them hanging on. But that's what God wants us to do sometimes. When things are out of our control, we are asked to wait and trust and hope and pray. When our problems grow too big, we have to rely on the strength of God and trust that even while our worlds might not come out unscathed, he will be with us—no matter what. And when the credits roll, we'll realize that all we needed was God all along.

MORAL MONSTERS

Godzilla, at first, was a terror of the atomic age (itself a terror the Japanese knew better than most). Later, he became a protector, fighting other symbolic horrors: Mechagodzilla and the inhuman technology it represented; the Smog Monster and the inherent environmental message it brought. The latest Godzilla movie had an environmental message too. Director Gareth Edwards told *The Daily Beast* that M.U.T.O.s represented "man's abuse of nature." They are uncovered in a hasty uranium strip mine operation and find refuge in nuclear facilities.

Many, if not most, of our monsters have always been highly symbolic. Werewolves could be seen as the beast within all of us, vampires our undead hungers and lusts, dragons our greed . . . our cinematic monsters are sometimes like Rorschach tests with popcorn. These are *our* monsters. The same things vanquished on-screen often represent the challenges and terrors of our own lives.

But sometimes these monsters—as frightening as they are— can take even our desire for justice and fairness and twist it beyond recognition. Some of these creatures are strangely, frighteningly *moral*. They dole out terminal punishment to those who lie, cheat, drink too much, or sleep around. "The wages of sin is death," Paul tells us in Romans 6:23. "And guess what?" monster movies add. "It's payday!"

Slasher movies, with their supernaturally tinged masked monsters, are the most obvious example. In the original *Halloween*, Michael Myers kills everyone who has sex, while virginal Laurie Strode (Jamie Lee Curtis) survives. In the approximately three quintillion *Friday the 13th* movies, Jason Voorhees and his mother (both of whom died, technically, because of drunk, randy teens) seem to have it out for anyone who breaks a commandment. The trope is so strong and so consistent that this "sin clause" was called out in 1996's *Scream*.

Rule "number one," the character Randy tells his audience. "You can never have sex. . . . Sex equals death, OK? Number two: You can never drink or do drugs."

But it's not just slasher flicks that hold true to this twisted sense of justice. Most monster movies will make evil characters—or even annoying ones—pay. Who is *Jaws*'s very first victim? Chrissie, a possibly drunk, high, or otherwise chemically impaired girl who goes skinny dipping with a guy. Who gets devoured by a venom-spitting dinosaur in *Jurassic Park*? Dennis, the DNA-stealing computer dude.

Oh, sure, nice people get killed and eaten at times too. They have to. Moviemakers don't want to confuse viewers as to who the real bad guy is. But it's clear that sin attracts monsters like Donald Sterling attracts lawyers. And often, our most virtuous characters—those who love their family and friends, and those who risk everything for them—wind up being our heroes. Dr. Alan Grant didn't survive the rigors of *Jurassic Park* just because of his paleontology expertise; he made it as a reward for taking such good care of John Hammond's two grandkids. In *Jaws*, why does Martin Brody survive the shark's attack aboard the *Orca* while Captain Quint goes down with his, er, fish? Martin's a loving father, that's why; Quint, the gruff loner, was so acidic that he probably gave Jaws a little indigestion. (At least, for the short time the shark lived afterward.)

Of course, that's the way we want it to work in our stories. We want the good guys to survive and the bad guys to get their due. That's Storytelling 101. But it also speaks to an ingrained, even biblical sense of justice. Again, there are echoes of universal right and wrong here—and the belief that the universe itself (in the guise of these horrifically imperfect executioners) will punish wrongdoers.

But sometimes, clean living just ain't enough. Some monsters, rather than giving the good guys a pass, want to stick it to the hero, corrupt the heroine, and drag everyone down to hell. And that's when the movies call in reinforcements.

A LITTLE HELP DOWN HERE?

The Lord of the Rings movies had some pretty great monsters. But none, in my opinion, was cooler than the Balrog in *The Fellowship of the Ring*. The flames, the whip, the snort-smoke action he's got going on. . . . For me, that five-minute scene with the Balrog was worth a full-price ticket (and a box of Jujubes too). When something's scary enough to chase off a gazillion goblins and so fearsome as to make even Gandalf go pale, you know this is not a fellow to be trifled with.

"Swords are no more use here!" Gandalf tells Aragorn.

But the wily old wizard has a trick or two left to play.

"You cannot pass!" Gandalf bellows at the beast. "I am a servant of the Secret Fire, wielder of the flame of Anor. The dark fire will not avail you, flame of Udûn! Go back to the Shadow! *You shall not pass!*"

Now, prepare to get geeky.

Anor, I'm told, is the Elvish word for "sun," and the "Secret Fire" is perhaps a reference to God (known in Tolkien's works as *Eru Ilúvatar*). And *Udûn* is a Middle-earth word for the underworld.

So this encounter wasn't just an opportunity for director Peter Jackson to flex his CGI muscles; this was a cinematic showdown between heaven and hell. An *exorcism*. Gandalf was trying to cast the Balrog "back to the Shadow" from whence it came. Yes, the Balrog eventually caught Gandalf with his flaming whip. But that only adds to the power of the story. The wizard stared down evil itself and gave his life both for his friends and for the world itself . . . and rose again in the very next movie. You probably don't need to read this book to get the potent symbolism in *that*.

TURN TOWARD THE LIGHT

In our more secular age, of course, our cinematic monsters wouldn't always be put off by an impassioned wizard. They don't always cower at the sign of a cross anymore, nor are they always vanquished by pure virtue. And sometimes, they don't lose at all. As of this writing, that demon in the *Paranormal Activity* series continues to plague suburban amateur filmmakers everywhere.

But even now, when it comes to real monsters of darkness, many time-honored tropes are still in play. Monsters haunt the night and melt away in the day. They're seen as supernatural entities, beyond the realm of science and reason—and those who rely too heavily on rationalism often are fatally unprepared. And those who dare face them are, generally, "good" people (however the movie defines *good*).

Yeah, horror movies with demons, spooks, and things that go bump in the night are dark and, by definition, occultic—nonstarters for many a Christian cinephile. And yet, it's in these very movies where the power of faith is explicitly at work. These stories tell us, as the apostle Paul does, that "we do not wrestle against flesh and blood, but against the rulers, against the authorities, against the cosmic powers over this present darkness" (Eph. 6:12 ESV).

We see lots of evidence of this present darkness in *The Conjuring*, a 2013 fright flick based on an allegedly true story. It centers around the Perron family—husband Roger, wife Carolyn, and their five daughters—who move into a huge and quite creepy old farmhouse that is, alas, still home to a century-old witch/demon named Bathsheba. The Perrons have barely finished unpacking before Bathsheba starts killing pets, clapping her hands in wardrobes, and dragging the girls around by the hair. And when Bible-believing paranormal investigators Ed and Lorraine Warren start to investigate, they find something even more disturbing: when alive, Bathsheba sacrificed her own newborn baby to Satan and, as such, likes to possess mothers and force them to kill their own children.

No surprise, then, that it takes over Carolyn and prepares to sacrifice two of the daughters.

The Warrens attempt an exorcism in the black of night, in a basement thick with old sins and sharp tools. The demon inside spits blood and howls in pain, but still it clings to Carolyn's soul. And when it hears a little girl in the bowels of the house, Bathsheba, still controlling Carolyn, makes a break for it—snatching the girl and carrying her into a cave-like, near-unreachable space, preparing to plunge scissors into the child's breast.

"Bathsheba!" Ed Warren shouts. "By the power of God, I condemn you back to hell!"

And then Lorraine, straining to touch Carolyn's head—almost in a gesture of blessing—asks the mother, the real mother inside, to remember a precious memory—a day at the beach, the dunes bathed in sunlight, and her children running and laughing under the blue, beautiful sky.

"Remember that day you said you'd never forget," Lorraine tells her. "You said they meant the world to you."

The sun rises. The light falls across Carolyn's gray, bloodstained face. And she cries. The nightmare is over and the monster is gone, destroyed through virtue and light, through faith and love.

"If I speak in tongues of human beings and of angels but I don't have love, I'm a clanging gong or a clashing cymbal," Paul wrote. "If I have the gift of prophecy and I know all the mysteries and everything else, and if I have such complete faith that I can move mountains but I don't have love, I'm nothing. If I give away everything that I have and hand over my own body to feel good about what I've done but I don't have love, I receive no benefit whatsoever" (1 Cor. 13:1-3).

Love, as Paul writes later, abides along with faith and hope; and love, he says, is the greatest of these on earth or in heaven. It is able to break through the gates of hell and conquer the most monstrous of monsters. Love saved Carolyn's daughter. It saved Carolyn. It can save us all.

And maybe it already has.

THINGS THAT GO BUMP IN THE LIGHT

Monsters are frightening things, particularly the ones that hide. We all have monsters in our lives—the things that terrify us, that torture us, that turn us into something we're not. We battle them every day. I do, at least. There are times I struggle with depression, procrastination, distraction, and doubt. I'm facing a monster even now. To write—to string words together as I do, and lay bare thoughts and feelings—can itself be a frightening thing. There are days that this computer screen can seem as daunting as a dragon.

But it's through these monsters that we learn to persevere. We fight when we must. We see the value of living like we ought. We lean on God as we should. When darkness comes we turn toward the light. Because in the light—the bright spark of God's love—the monsters go away.

CHAPTER 5
SOMETHING'S ROTTING
IN DENMARK

Being Born Again . . . the Zombie Way

Don't you know what's goin' on out there?
This is no Sunday school picnic!
—Ben (Duane Jones), *Night of the Living Dead*

Z ombies look horrible in evening wear. They're prone to having their noses fall off at the most inopportune times. You can't have them over for a nice dinner for fear they'd eat the cook. You'll rarely see them do a talk show, either: they're notoriously abysmal interviews.

Perky hostess: "We're here with Mr. Reginald Ermortis, who has written a delightfully short book titled *Shambles: My Dead, Dead, Dead Life*. Reg, why don't you tell us why, after twenty successful years of eating brains, you decided to turn your attention to writing?"

Reg: "Aaaaoouuuughhh."

Hostess: "Well, isn't that interesting! I thought as much. Now, on page 23 of your book, you say—wait, is that your *nose*...?"

Nevertheless, zombies are all the rage in the entertainment industry, and they have been for years. They have been behind blockbuster movies (*World War Z*), outrageously successful television shows (AMC's *The Walking Dead*), best-selling books (Seth Grahame-Smith's *Pride and Prejudice and Zombies*), smash pop hits (anything by Miley Cyrus) and 80 percent of the video games ever made (*The Last Of Us, Resident Evil, Left 4 Dead, LittleBigPlanet: The Corpseworld,* and so on, and so on). You can buy zombie defense kits (Crosslinks's "3-Day Defense Survival Kit" comes with food, glowsticks, and a blanket, though curiously no chainsaw), go to zombie conventions (Seattle's 2013 ZomBCon was labeled as "The World's Largest Zombie Culture Convention & Survival Expo") and take part in zombie runs (as either the sprinting living or the shambling dead, giving new meaning to "running your feet off"). When Discovery's *Mythbusters* dedicates a whole show to zombies, you know the genre's a big deal.

Why dedicate a whole chapter to these "unmentionables," as Elizabeth calls them in Seth Grahame-Smith's *Pride and Prejudice and Zombies*? We could've already (*ahem*) buried them earlier in chapters 3 or 4, as they're technically monsters that can trigger the end of the world. Zombies put the "Arrrgghhh" in Armageddon, so to speak, and as we'll see, they're way more probable, biblically speaking, than some magnetic pole-shifting anomaly (please stand up, *2012*).

But that's just the thing. Zombies have lessons all their own to teach us—and deeply spiritual ones, at that.

"PLEASE TURN TO ZOMBIRIAH, CHAPTER 2, VERSE 4 . . . "

Yeah, that's right: zombies are biblical. Sort of.

In Revelation—as apocalyptic a book as there is in the Bible—a couple of hombres are killed and are left in the middle of town, presumably to feed the local magpies. But then, after three-and-a-half days of lying in the sun or rain or what have you, they get up and scare the stuffing out of passersby (Rev. 11:1-14). The Bible doesn't say they ate anyone's brains or grunted a lot, but neither does it say they were "normal," either. And given the fact they had a good few days to decay before they rose again and were snatched up into heaven, I can't imagine they looked too pretty by then.

Or then there's this charming vision of the future, courtesy of that hip prophet of yore, Zechariah:

> This is the plague with which the LORD will strike all the nations that fought against Jerusalem [when Jesus comes for a second time]: Their flesh will rot while they are still standing on their feet, their eyes will rot in their sockets, and their tongues will rot in their mouths. (Zech. 14:12-13 NIV, adapted)

Zechariah, you'll recall, lived and (we hope) died a good 2,500 years ago—far too early to see an advance copy of *Day of the Dead* or something. And these shambling, decaying mounds of flesh arrive just in time for Christ's second coming.

"But wait," careful and annoying readers might be thinking. "Those aren't zombies. Zechariah never said these rotting people were actually *dead*. And if corpses don't catch colds, they certainly wouldn't catch plagues."

Good observation, my dear reader (if you're both careful and annoying)! Give yourself a gold star. But that shows how little you understand about modern zombie scholarship. The actual life-status of zombies is a matter of some debate.

In truth, zombie experts squabble over the exact nature of the undead like preschoolers over the last available Sit 'n Spin. Which forces us to ask a series of unseemly but important questions:

Are zombies alive or dead?

Are they alive *and* dead?

Are some alive and some dead?

Would the dead ones mingle with the live ones at parties? Or would they fight like the Jets and Sharks from *West Side Story*, only with far more awkward dance numbers?

Our entertainment seems to be split on the question. In *Pride and Prejudice and Zombies*, the demure but battle-seasoned protagonist Elizabeth is often called upon to behead some of the countryside's recently buried (i.e., fully dead) "unmentionables" while keeping her honor—and corset—in place. George Romero's zombies from his many horror movies (including *Night of the Living Dead*) and the "walkers" from *The Walking Dead* (both the comics and the AMC TV series) are zombies of this order. Sure, they once were your friends and neighbors, but their souls flew the coop a long time ago; now they're just animated lumps of human-looking jelly—like *Pirates of the Caribbean* animatronics designed by Walt Disney's very disturbed younger cousin.

But movies such as *28 Days Later* and games such as *Left 4 Dead* contend that zombies are only, in the words of *The Princess Bride*'s Miracle Max, *"mostly* dead." Sure, they've been better. Maybe their hearts have stopped beating and their lungs have stopped working and their brains have all the reasoning power of a particularly aggressive form of kumquat. But these zombies never truly died. They just changed—thanks to a particularly nasty, highly contagious disease. Max Brooks, in his best-selling *The Zombie Survival Guide,* insists the root of zombie-ism is the mysterious Solanum virus, which terminates all bodily functions and remakes the brain into a flesh-seeking homing device. "Solanum does *not* create life," Brooks informs us, "it alters it."

So in some ways, zombification isn't really a question of being alive or dead. It depends on how you define it.

NOT DEAD YET

R is dead in 2013's *Warm Bodies*. No doubt about it. We know it. He knows it. *Why can't I connect with people?* he thinks to himself early on. *Oh, right, it's because I'm dead.* No one, and I mean no one, is more dead than R.

He's so dead that the only joy he gets out of life—er, *death*—is eating brains. He loves 'em like I love lemon meringue pie (and to my sudden horror, I'd imagine both have the same sort of consistency). But it's not just because brains taste so yummy. In fact, that's only part of the charm of snacking on cerebellum. R and other zombies like brains because, somehow, eating them allows them to tap into their victims' memories. They, in a sense, "remember" what it was like to be alive.

R finds romantic interest Julie through this very method—by devouring Julie's ex-boyfriend. Sure, it's one of the more awkward ways to meet girls, but it works. She's not like all the other live, screaming victims he's come across. He likes her. He wants to protect her from all his dead-end friends. And slowly, against some fairly staggering odds, the two grow close.

And here's the really weird thing: R stops being so dead. He gets warmer. His grunts become words. He stops obsessing so much about brains. Slowly, gradually, R lurches back to life.

Which, when you think about it, is exactly what happens when we become Christians. And in a way, zombies themselves could be seen as a profound spiritual metaphor.

No, no. Don't close this book. Not yet, anyway. Just hear me out.

LIVING THE DREAM

Even setting aside Zechariah, the Bible talks a lot about life after death. We hear a little about heaven and hell. We read lots of stories of people physically raised from the dead: the prophet Elijah brought a boy back to life with heartfelt prayer and some strange calisthenics ("he stretched himself out on the boy three times," we're told in 1 Kings 17:21 NIV). Elisha, Elijah's understudy, resurrected two people—including one after the prophet was just a pile of bones himself. ("When the body touched Elisha's bones, the man came to life and stood up on his feet," according to 2 Kings 13:21 NIV.) Peter and Paul both successfully brought people back to life. Jesus, of course, returned no fewer than three folks to the land of the living—and, as an encore, he engineered his own resurrection for good measure.

But here's the thing: none of them were zombies. They were really, truly *alive* again. Because when God reanimates your whole being, there's no need to watch for shedding body parts. The Bible tells us that one of them even sneezed seven times after being raised. It's a well-known fact that traditional zombies (being both immune to colds and resistant to seasonal allergies) don't sneeze.

But the Bible's just getting (*ahem*) warmed up on the subject. See, the Scriptures don't talk just about literal death, but also spiritual death—which is defined as our being separated from God through sin. If there's anything that'll get Paul to writing, it's this very subject.

"At one time you were like a dead person because of the things you did wrong and your offenses against God," he tells the Ephesians (2:1). "When you were dead because of the things you had done wrong and because your body wasn't circumcised, God made you alive with Christ and forgave all the things you had done wrong," he writes to the Colossians (2:13). "The wages that sin pays are death, but God's gift is eternal life in Christ Jesus our Lord," he says to the Romans (6:23). Sure, Paul is talking about eternal life in this last example, but I think he's also talking about having life *now*. Because without God, we're dead.

Like zombies.

When we look at R before he met Julie, you find someone going through the motions of life but not really alive. He'd shamble about from place to place, rudderless. "I'm lonely," he admits to himself. "I'm totally lost. I mean, I'm literally lost. I've never been in this part of the airport before."

That, to me, is life without God: we don't know why we're here. We don't know what we're supposed to do. We wind up feeling like we're alone. Lost—sometimes literally, given our lack of direction. We feel empty inside. Dead. Apart from God, we may live—and yet we don't. We pretend. We can be, in a sense, zombies. We might not snack on people's calves, but we suffer all the same.

Even the zombie's penchant for brains makes sense. R desires to consume the memories of his victim in order to feel alive again. In another zombie flick, *Return of the Living Dead*, a zombie actually tells somebody that her kin eat brains to deal with the pain.

"What about the pain?" her inquisitor asks.

Her reply: "The pain of being DEAD!"

Eating brains is something of an analgesic for them, then— something to ease the pain and feel alive. Which, when you think about it, is how many of us humans use things in our own walks: drinking, using drugs, dabbling in porn, searching for unhealthy thrills, or engaging in any number of sins and addictions to take away the pain—things that many claim "make me feel alive."

But as R knows, and as we all really understand too, whatever we engage in—be it brains or otherwise—is at best a temporary fix. The core deadness inside of us can't be resurrected through another glass of beer, no matter how nicely crafted it is, or through another raise, no matter how well deserved it might be.

The only thing that can make us live again is love. And, with all due respect to R and Julie, it has to be God's love. To truly live means more than being in possession of a beating heart and a working set of lungs: it's about being in communion with God himself. For when we're apart from God, we really don't know much about life—true life—at all.

But sometimes, even when we have life, we can lose sight of the monsters we can be.

GOOD MONSTERS?

"I also have always liked the monster-within idea," zombie godfather George A. Romero told AMC. "I like the zombies being us."

Yeah, zombies are monsters. No doubt about it. They don't walk like us, talk like us (if at all), and their penchant to eat us is troubling. But if we watch a lot of zombie entertainment (and I wouldn't recommend it), we'll find that, sometimes, the zombies are the least of humanity's problems.

Romero and others have used the creatures as shambling metaphors—said to reference everything from communism to racism to, I don't know, our penchant for talk radio. When Romero sent the living dead to a mall in 1978's *Dawn of the Dead*, he wasn't just interested in how zombies dealt with escalators. He meant it to be a reflection on our own sometimes mindless attitudes toward disposable consumer goods. Sometimes when we see these mindless menaces shamble around on city streets, we see how mindless we can all be. Or so goes the theory.

At times, the zombies seem ironically more humane than our human heroes—or at least, less cruel. You don't need to watch AMC's *The Walking Dead* for long to realize that the series's real monsters aren't them; they're us.

In *The Walking Dead* everyone, alive or dead, is already infected with a serious zombie virus: it's just that they don't get sick (as it were) until they die. So keep that in mind while you read the next part.

In the final episode of season 3, the Governor—a ruthless leader of a band of survivors—orders his one-time loyal lieutenant, Milton, to kill a woman handcuffed to a dental chair. When Milton makes an attempt to assassinate the Governor instead, the leader stabs him several times and leaves him on the ground to die. And then return.

"I told you to kill her but you didn't," the Governor says. "And now you gonna turn and you gonna tear away the flesh of her bones. In this life now you kill or you die. Or you die and you kill."

Now, who's the real monster here?

The zombies in *The Walking Dead* force humanity to the edge, and what we reveal of ourselves there isn't often pretty. See, zombies kill without really thinking about it. They kill because that's what they're programmed to do. They're like sharks in that way—very slow, bipedal sharks. And while you certainly can do your best to keep yourself out of a shark's tummy, you can't really blame the beast for wanting to eat you. It's not like it has some sort of evil vendetta (unless you count 1987's *Jaws: The Revenge*).

But men and women, we often purposefully do wrong. And we do, often. We can hurt out of malice and spite, out of passion or disinterest. And sometimes, we can even hurt with the best of intentions.

I AM MISTAKEN

In the 2007 movie *I Am Legend*, protagonist Dr. Robert Neville is the ultimate loner, and not by choice. Years before, a man-made virus tore through civilization and killed almost everyone, which was bad enough. Even worse, most of the survivors have turned into zombie/vampire-like creatures (called Darkseekers) who hate the sun and love human flesh (a truly rare delicacy these days). For a good (*ahem*) chunk of the movie, Robert—immune to the disease—believes he might be the only living human in New York, and possibly the world. And he spends part of his time studying the creatures, as an anthropologist or visiting alien might.

"An infected male exposed himself to sunlight today," Robert tells his audio journal. "Now it's possible decreased brain function or growing scarcity of food is causing them to . . . ignore their basic survival instincts. Social de-evolution appears complete. Typical human behavior is now entirely absent."

But Robert, being a doctor and all, hasn't completely lost hope. These zombies are only *mostly* dead. Maybe with a lot of hard work, a little luck, and not a small amount of zombie blood, he can find a vaccine, or even a cure, for this horrific disease. So Robert goes out hunting: he bags live zombies and totes them back to his laboratory, killing any errant Darkseekers who might threaten him. Once he gets his subject safely back, he injects potential serums that might—just *might*—cure the poor guy or gal. Sure, the serums tend to kill the zombies (again?), but you can't rebuild civilization without bending a few nails, right?

In the end, Neville's perseverance and courage save the day. While fiddling with a female Darkseeker he recently captured, he discovers his latest serum seems to be working. He entrusts the formula to a woman named Anna he miraculously just met (New York really *is* a magical place), then blows himself up before he can be killed and digested by the Darkseekers' unhinged leader—the same guy who lunged at him in the sunlight—and his pack of pale buddies.

"Dr. Robert Neville dedicated his life to the discovery of a cure and the restoration of humanity," we're told in the end. "On September 9th, 2012, at approximately 8:49 p.m., he discovered that cure. And at 8:52, he gave his life to defend it. We are his legacy. This is his legend. Light up the darkness."

Which is all great! Way to go, sacrificial Robert! It's another Christ metaphor!

Except that it's kinda bull.

Imagine *you're* the big, bad Darkseeker—Eugene, we'll call you. One afternoon, you and your pals are snoozing away in the warehouse y'all call home, when suddenly this dude comes around—a known killer—and captures your main squeeze, coldcocking her with a rifle butt to knock the poor thing out. Then this guy (clearly a real psychopathic jerk) hightails back to his nefarious lair with your girlfriend. And while you don't know exactly where the lair is or what he's up to, you know that he's done it before—*and no one's ever returned.*

No wonder you, Eugene, get irate. Wouldn't you risk a little sunlight to save your delicate flower? Why, for all you know, he might be conducting loathsome experiments on her (and you'd be right). Why *wouldn't* you get your pals together to rescue her?

Didn't Luke Skywalker do the very same thing when Darth Vader kidnapped Princess Leia? Didn't Mario give it his all to save Princess Peach, repeatedly, from Bowser? Why would you do anything less for your own pigment-deprived princess?

I Am Legend's original ending—one apparently detested by test audiences—helped us see the situation more clearly from Eugene's point of view. Instead of hurtling himself mindlessly into the Plexiglass panel separating him from Robert and Eugene's trapped girlfriend, Eugene smears a butterfly on the glass instead. Robert realizes he's seen that butterfly before . . . tattooed on the shoulder of Eugene's lady. Apparently, these zombies aren't so, um, brainless after all, Robert realizes. He stops trying to fix the, er, woman, unlocks the Plexiglass, and wheels her out to Eugene, who takes her away (rescues her). No explosion, no grand sacrifice—just a reminder that the world, even one filled with zombies, is more complex than it might seem.

That's a whole lot closer to the point of Richard Matheson's book *I Am Legend*, which ends with Robert admitting that, to these people—this new and very different civilization—*he* is the monster, "a new superstition entering the unassailable fortress of forever. I am legend."

With *I Am Legend*, we again see hints of what it means to be Christian in a secular world. Only *these* hints are a little less flattering.

ENGAGING OUR BRRRAAAAIIIINNNNS!

If we're Christian, we've been given life, it is true. True, glorious, and eternal life. The Bible makes it clear. Understandably, we want to share that life with those around us. Heck, that's what we're *called* to do. We've been given a gift, the greatest gift of all. And we long to give it to others. When we follow Christ we fall in love. And everyone in love wants the world to feel just as happy.

But—and I say this from personal experience—people who are deliriously in love can also be incredibly annoying to those who aren't. In high school, if I had just gone through a messy breakup, the last thing I'd want to hear about (much less spend hours upon hours talking about) is how in love one of my friends might be. "Nothing like being in love," they might tell me. "You should try it sometime!"

Yeah, that's almost like an invitation for a punch in the nose.

We Christians, I think, can fall prey to the same dynamics. We talk about how wonderful God is to someone who might've had a real bad experience in a church. We might speak about "God's truth" to someone who isn't yet convinced that God is even real. We know that our non-Christian friends need God, which they do; it's so obvious to us. And so we try to fix them, like Robert does, without asking whether they're ready to be fixed. We sometimes jump into their lives uninvited. Sometimes unwanted.

And then the divisions between us spread. We grow impatient with an unbeliever's skepticism. We openly lament their sins. We become exasperated by their lack of faith.

Maybe they look at us and see moralism. Legalism. Inconsistency in what we say versus how we act. In our efforts to do the right thing—to fix something that clearly needs to be fixed—we begin to obscure the love and grace of God, which is the only fixin' glue we have.

In 2007, the Barna Group polled sixteen- to twenty-nine-year-olds and found that only 16 percent of unbelievers in this age group had a "good impression" of Christianity. A lowly 3 percent had a favorable opinion of evangelical Christians, the faith's most visible American branch. About 87 percent of those unbelievers said that Christians were judgmental, and 85 percent said they were hypocritical. And the evangelicals polled? More than 9 out of 10 believed that "Americans are becoming more hostile and negative toward Christianity."

That kind of mutual distrust leads to more misunderstandings, more clashes. Extremists from both sides stoke the rhetorical fires. And so we draw hard lines between *us* and *them*: children of God versus condemned and hateful heathens. Enlightened, rational freethinkers versus superstitious, bigoted Christians.

Humans versus zombies. And who you consider the zombies to be depends, I suppose, on where you stand.

It's funny. In some ways, it seems like we Christians have taken the metaphor a little too seriously. I know Christians who work for Christian organizations, send their kids to Christian schools, frequent nothing but Christian businesses, see nothing but Christian movies, listen to nothing but Christian music. . . . They might spend the rest of their lives sequestered in a purely traditional Christian world—as if contact with whatever lies outside those protective Christian walls might be catching. We have a tendency to lock ourselves away, worried that atheism and humanism might at any minute relentlessly pound on our doors in search of our brains.

Yeah, the world outside the Christian bubble can be a little frightening. But that said, I don't think we have any reason to fear. Not if we know the truth. Not if we carry God's love.

Look at the contrast again between *Warm Bodies* and *I Am Legend*. In the first case, R is drawn by love. In the second, "Eugene" is repelled by a frightening being who attacks and takes. Eugene does not understand, and no wonder: our hero, Robert, never bothers to explain.

"There is no fear in love, but perfect love drives out fear," we read in 1 John 4:18, "because fear expects punishment. The person who is afraid has not been made perfect in love."

In *I Am Legend*, Robert is looking to literally save mankind. And yet, to those he's trying to save, his actions look like fear. In *Warm Bodies*, Julie isn't trying to save anybody—not initially. And yet R is drawn to her. He is drawn by love.

And here's another interesting verse for you out of 1 John again, just one chapter before: "We know that we have transferred from death to life, because we love the brothers and sisters. The person who does not love remains in death" (3:14).

Clearly, John knew something about the living dead.

We love our entertainment-based zombies. They are, in many ways, reflections of us. But as Christians, it's important that they don't reflect us too much. And the only way to walk out of that lurching look of death is to embrace not only life, but love.

CHAPTER 6

DRAWN OF A NEW DAY

Animated Movies and the Problem of Pain

We trailed him to a little dive down on Yukster Street. We went in. Only he got the drop on us, literally. Dropped a piano on us from fifteen stories. Broke my arm, Teddy never made it. I never did find out who that guy was. All I remember was him standing over me laughing, with those burning red eyes, and that high, squeaky voice.

—Eddie Valiant (Bob Hoskins), *Who Framed Roger Rabbit?*

It's been a bleak ride through the entertainment industry thus far. We've stalked through the bitter, brooding minds of superheroes. We've run with the zombies. We've stared down our monsters and watched as the earth was all but destroyed several times over. Yes, Hollywood does indeed offer some redemptive messages throughout all this nigh-annihilation, but we cannot ignore that the collateral damage has been high. Countless extras have faked their deaths to bring these hints of hope to you. Hundreds of CGI cities have burned to the CGI ground. Now you know the awful truth: theater popcorn is buttered with tears.

But all of this death and destruction was mere prelude to the grittier, grim world to which we now travel. We must dive into a genre filled with terrible deeds and cold hearts, where grief is as sharp as a dragon's tooth, where betrayal and pain pour through like water.

I speak of cartoons.

Or, more fairly, animated movies. Cartoons are what I used to watch on Saturday morning—a boy in my footie pajamas, watching whatever schlock Hanna-Barbera wished to feed us impressionable youngsters that season. *Captain Caveman*? Awesome. *Jabberjaw*? Radical. *The Herculoids*? I ate it up like a bowl of Cheerios and begged, sometimes literally, for more. (My parents could be quite strict about my TV time.)

Today's animated movies are as close to Saturday morning cartoons as *Anna Karenina* is to *The Pokey Little Puppy*.

"You have to write the book that wants to be written," Madeleine L'Engle once wrote. "And if the book will be too difficult for grown-ups, then you write it for children." I think that's true for movies too. Animated films may be filled with talking animals and slapstick humor, but the stories themselves are often quite mature and, sometimes, really difficult to make it through without a tissue. I don't know if there's ever been a sadder movie moment than when Bambi realizes his mother's gone. And don't tell me your eyes didn't get a little blurry when Mufasa met his fate in *The Lion King*. Today—in what's become a glorious second Golden Age for animated features—these "cartoons" are among the most moving, most poignant stories told onscreen. I can chuckle through a disaster movie, roll my eyes through a monster flick. But make a few action figures come to life and send them on a quest for love and meaning (I'm looking at you, *Toy Story 1, 2,* and *3*), and I'm a mess at the end. Five-year-olds have to console *me*. "It's OK," they might say. "It's not real, you know."

I think these wise five-year-olds know a dirty little secret: while animated flicks may spawn a bazillion Happy Meal toys and inspire a library's worth of coloring books, many seem to be written for folks who've grown out of their juice boxes. I mean, think about Disney/Pixar's *Up* for a minute: What *kids'* movie would feature a cranky septuagenarian widower as its main hero? Hanna-Barbera never would've allowed something like that on its watch.

Animated movies have grown up. And just like life, they're filled with a bittersweet beauty and the problem of pain. They deal with love and loss, insecurity and grief. And even though they give us worlds that have never been and can never be, the emotions on which they draw are universal, familiar to the youngest and oldest of us.

Animated movies don't shy away from pain. Angst is a part of their stories, just as it is in ours. But these flicks don't just acknowledge the reality of discomfort: they tell us, just as the Bible does, that there's sometimes purpose behind the pain. There are reasons for it. Lessons to be learned through it. And they can help us see, through the lens of movies, what is so often hidden from us in real life: that even in the midst of pain, we don't walk alone.

GRUING THE DAY

Gru, the pointy-nosed, turtleneck-bedecked "hero" of the *Despicable Me* movies, knows all about pain. Hey, the dude *is* a pain, at least at first. If there's a balloon, he'll pop it. If there's an ice cream cone, he'll steal it. He's the type of guy who'd swipe money from the collection plate (if he ever went to church) or stiff the waitress at Village Inn (if he ever chewed on anything besides bitterness). He's a card-carrying member of the National Villainy Association, and he wants nothing more than to be the GREATEST (WORST?) BAD GUY THE WORLD HAS EVER SEEN! (Cue diabolical laughter and some ominous orchestral music here, please.)

Or at least, so ran the plan. Until he experienced a little pain himself in the form of three little orphan girls selling cookies.

Oh, you may think that it was love that triggered Gru's better instincts in Illumination Entertainment and Universal Pictures's *Despicable Me*. And it was. But how did that manifest itself most often? Pain. The sort of pain that only little children can inflict.

Consider that Gru, before these children came along, was happy. Well, relatively speaking. Yes, clearly he had some unresolved issues with his mother. But it's not like he longed for additional companionship. He had his minions. He had his colleague Dr. Nefario. He had his . . . fang-laden beast, whatever it is. But for the most part, he was quite content to steal Vegas properties and the occasional orbiting planetoid. Initially, the kids—Margo, Edith, and Agnes—were just tools in Gru's nefarious master plan. He'd use the children to steal a shrink ray (he told himself) and abandon them right after.

But then he discovers what most parents quickly learn: kids can be a pain. When he's making a presentation to drum up funds for his moon-stealing project, they sneak in a drawing of him sitting on a toilet (how embarrassing). They squirrel away his precious plotting time (how aggravating). And after a successful shrink-ray heist, the girls nag Gru into an amusement-park visit—where he promptly gets sick (how . . . messy). The girls are the zenith of aggravation—an element of painful chaos in Gru's once-orderly world. His whole relationship with them is filled with discomfort and annoyances and pain.

And, again like most parents, he comes to realize that he kinda likes it.

No, it's not like Gru discovers the masochist in him. But he grows to understand that he *loves* those girls. And when you love somebody, you know the relationship will involve a certain amount of pain.

I know this sounds a little counterintuitive. We don't like pain. We mostly run from it, in fact, and we expect that our loved ones will help keep the pain away. And, of course, they do.

But at the same time, I think there's a certain amount of weirdness in any worthwhile relationship—moments of discomfort that must be overcome for the relationship to continue. Sometimes these moments are products of shared adventure, like Gru's experience at the amusement park. We take part in an activity because someone we love asks us to. And yet, through these moments of minor pain, we still grow mysteriously closer (even if we stress that, no matter how much you love your Aunt Edna, you're never, ever skydiving with her again).

But sometimes, relationships are a source of *real* pain. Something is said that can't be taken back. Someone does something they shouldn't. Someone doesn't do something they should. We hurt. We cause hurt. We try to say sorry, but we can't. We want to forgive, but the pain gets in the way.

These things can destroy a relationship, of course. And when a friendship or a romance or even a bond between parent and child breaks, it's almost always the result of pain like this. We've been hurt too much or too often.

But sometimes when we inflict or suffer these sorts of really awful wounds, they serve as a catalyst to a better, stronger relationship. Really. And in the case of *Despicable Me*, it's pain like this that helped make Gru a whole lot less . . . despicable.

No matter how often his adopted kids draw on his walls or pester him for bedtime stories, our villainous hero gets closer to them with each passing day. But he still has hopes to steal the moon, too—and the optimal time for moon-stealing runs smack-dab into the kids' dance recital (and trust me, dance recitals can be as painful as anything). The children are becoming a distraction, Dr. Nefario huffs. "If you don't do something about them, then I will." So Gru reluctantly turns them back over to the orphanage.

Gru, naturally, succeeds in his titanic, tidal-destroying plan. He shrinks the moon to the size of a softball and begins the trip home. But then Gru sees his recital ticket floating away, and he realizes—in the midst of his own pain and guilt—that the moon is really just a big ol' rock. It's nothing compared to the love of his three little girls.

So when Gru puts the moon back in place and everything's again right with the world, he tries to make it right with his girls—

rescued from the orphanage—in the most face-saving way he can think of: through a bedtime story.

"One big unicorn, strong and free, thought he was happy as he could be," Gru reads from his own book. "Then three little kittens came around and turned his whole life upside down. They made him laugh, they made him cry. He never should have said good-bye. And now he knows he can never part from those three little kittens that changed his heart."

Gru acknowledges in his story that even the best things (especially the best things) can be uncomfortable. Love can turn our lives upside down. Love can make us cry. Love can hurt. And yet in spite of that hurt—and sometimes because of it—we realize how precious love is, and how we'd do almost anything to have the opportunity to hurt for love.

When I think about love in the Bible—particularly the love between people and God—there's pain there. Jesus' disciples braved a great deal of discomfort, even to the point of death and beyond, because of their love for their risen leader. When Paul wrote that "the love of God has been poured out in our hearts through the Holy Spirit" (Rom. 5:5), he was in prison for preaching that very thing. John 3:16—the only verse that many of us actually know by heart—speaks of God's love for us, a love so deep that he gave up his Son for us. Think God can't feel pain? That verse wouldn't have much meaning if that sacrifice wasn't a horribly painful thing for God, and for Jesus, to do. "Love is patient, love is kind," Paul says (1 Cor. 13:4). But love isn't pain free. It can't be.

And I think that God sometimes uses pain to help us go the way we need to go.

HOME, SWEET . . . OH, NEVER MIND

The Croods, stars of DreamWorks Animation's 2013 film of the same name, put the *cave* in *caveman*: they depended on theirs like nobody's business. Never mind that home for this Paleolithic family was literally just a little hole in the wall—one that Eep, the Croods' teenage daughter, found a little confining. It still featured everything that paterfamilias Grug thought was important: granite countertops (and floors and ceilings and furniture); nice views of the dirt outside; a nice, private ledge where Eep could sulk. But most important for Grug, the Crood house was *safe*. If they rolled the door closed, nothing could get at them, no matter how long the claws, no matter how sharp the teeth, no matter how peevish the disposition. Yessir, while all their neighbors had long ago succumbed to poisonous serpents or rampaging mammoths or, who knows, bazooka-toting emus, the Croods had survived, thanks to their vault-like casa. Nothing, and I mean *nothing*, could shake them out of their home.

Unless it was the actual shaking of their home.

In fact, the whole region started shaking. And crumbling. And falling. In just a few indescribable seconds, their home was gone—crushed underneath a pile of rubble that once made a mountain. Even a thousand bazooka-toting emus couldn't have done that much damage so quickly. Just like that, the only security the Croods had ever known was gone.

That's the way things go sometimes, isn't it? We think everything is peachy until, without warning, it isn't. Life is like that old grenade Aunt Edna keeps in her attic for sentimental reasons. Sure, it looks safe, but you never know when it might go off.

The blows that hit us the hardest always seem to come when we're not looking for them: the unexpected death of a loved one, a sudden loss of employment, a lie revealed. And we feel, like the Croods, that our world has fallen around our ankles.

"Pain insists upon being attended to," C. S. Lewis wrote in his book *The Problem of Pain*. "God whispers to us in our pleasures, speaks in our consciences, but shouts in our pains. It is his megaphone to rouse a deaf world." We don't like to think that pain can ever be caused by God because we associate pain with evil. Pain is *bad*, we think. But that's not altogether true. Pain is *painful*, there's no question about that. But our bodies telegraph pain for some really good reasons. Pain keeps us away from touching hot griddles. It gives us a good, reasonable fear of rabid bears. It helps us know when to tag out when Aunt Edna gets us in one of those horrible headlocks of hers. That sort of pain—specifically, the fear of a painful death—kept the Croods safe in the cave for all those years. And that wasn't all bad.

But sometimes, pain tells us when it's time to move on. When it's time to get out of the cave and get busy with what God wants us to do. Pain can force us out of a rut and focus us on tomorrow. And in the case of *The Croods*, "Tomorrow" is an actual destination—"A place not like today, or yesterday," a new interloper named Guy tells this Cro-Magnon crew. "A place where things are better."

And so with the Croods' cave gone, they and Guy embark on a journey to Tomorrow—a trek filled with strange creatures and new experiences and, frankly, some significant moments of pain. But all those moments, bad and good, give them the wherewithal to push on.

It's a great lesson for us, I think. Sometimes the pain we feel in our lives is healthy. It's a warning we need to make a change, or a sign it's time to move on. Sometimes, the pain is a part of a change—a calling that we talked about a little earlier. Sometimes, I don't think God wants us to get too comfortable. When we're being challenged, we're forced into a place where we have to rely on him a little more. We have to trust. We have to push forward, hopefully in the direction God wants us to go.

The idea that pain sometimes can help us on our way is just one of *The Croods*'s cool lessons—a story so rich in little life metaphors that I'm tempted to go on. But maybe it's best to save them for *Burning Bush 2.1.* (Be sure to write my publisher and demand an extra-large advance for me.) So instead, let's quote another few-thousand-years-old guy named Paul, who sounds like he was on the road with Eep, Guy, et al., dodging saber-toothed kitties and the rest, before he settled down and penned this to the Romans:

> We rejoice in our sufferings, knowing that suffering produces endurance, and endurance produces character, and character produces hope, and hope does not put us to shame, because God's love has been poured into our hearts through the Holy Spirit who has been given to us. (Rom. 5:3-5 ESV)

The Croods suffered when their cave was crushed. But on the journey forced by that moment of pain, they found endurance.

They found character. And in the end, they found hope—hope for a better Tomorrow.

STUCK IN THE SKY

But sometimes, the pain is so great that tomorrow, and all our tomorrows, look gray and barren. We suffer. We endure. But hope is beyond us. Even faith can be hard. We wonder how a good God could allow such horrific, seemingly senseless pain.

In the world of entertainment, generally pain has purpose. Every hero needs to hurt to become that hero. We would not have heard of Katniss Everdeen without the Hunger Games. Batman wouldn't be Batman without the murder of his parents. These characters experienced horrible things that I'm sure they both would've rather not. And yet, these circumstances and events are integral to their journeys. Indeed, Paul's words echo in almost every heroic narrative: the titanic storm produces endurance. The bully beatdowns build character. More superficially, think of every training montage you've ever seen: Rocky huffing and puffing while running down the streets of Philadelphia. Bruce Wayne tangling with Henri Ducard in *Batman Begins*. Nacho being pelted with melons in *Nacho Libre*. No pain, no gain, we're told. Our suffering makes sense.

But animated movies tell a harder truth too—a truth too hard for the standard popcorn flick, a truth that children instinctively know: sometimes suffering doesn't make sense.

We don't like to think that children suffer, but of course they do. Friends become enemies for no reason. Siblings turn mean.

Parents divorce. Pets die. Promises break. Parents may try to instill a sense of cosmic karma in their kids—that good is forever rewarded, evil always punished. But children, sometimes more than adults, I think, see that not everything is just or fair in this world. People can be cruel. Life can be unfair. The ones we love can disappear forever.

I think of Bambi calling for his mother. Dumbo, separated from his mom by ugly, unfair bars. Elsa and Anna in *Frozen*, orphaned by pernicious seas and separated by a mysterious condition that wasn't either of their faults.

I think of *Up*, Disney/Pixar's 2009 masterpiece, and perhaps the most mature study of grief ever put onscreen.

Once upon a time, Carl Fredricksen fell in love with a girl named Ellie. She was adventurous, while he was cautious. She was full of life and color, while Carl stayed in sensible shades of brown. But they became friends nevertheless and, eventually, fell in love. And together they shared a dream of traveling to Paradise Falls—their own version of Guy's "Tomorrow," if you will.

But in a four-minute montage without dialogue, viewers watch as Carl and Ellie grow up and grow old. They build a life together full of Ellie's rainbow hues. They suffer along the way. They deal with problems—expensive ones that necessitate them dipping into their vacation fund again and again. Paradise Falls retreats into an ever-further tomorrow. And then after decades—when Carl finally decides to splurge to take the trip, the one dream they've always shared—Ellie gets sick. She dies.

It's as beautiful and painful a sequence as there is in cinema, I think, and if you're not reaching for a tissue by its end, you should see a doctor immediately and check that you've not been co-opted by a sinister galactic being. This isn't just sad: it's tragic and pointless and incredibly unfair. This isn't a superhero movie, where our protagonists die and spring from the grave at the least provocation. There's no possibility of time travel here, no chance that Carl can preserve Ellie's soul in a jar. She's gone. Their shared dreams are buried with her.

And the movie has barely even begun.

This isn't *Despicable Me*, where pain becomes a necessary catalyst for personal growth. It's not *The Croods*, wherein the destruction of today is necessary to find a better Tomorrow. There is no justification for a loss like this. The pain is not a catalyst. It just is. And it doesn't make sense.

We don't know whether Carl holds God responsible for the loss, as we might do in his shoes. But regardless, the guy (never a cuddly senior citizen to begin with) becomes a world-class crank. His post-Ellie motto might well be "Get off my lawn!" He clings so tightly to his memories of Ellie and all their yesterdays that he can't even see Tomorrow anymore. Even the outlandish dream he follows—to tie a bunch of balloons to his house and float to Paradise Falls—is rooted in a life that vanished with his soulmate. It's a bittersweet journey, emphasis on bitter. *Sure, Ellie can't see the Falls anymore*, Carl seems to acknowledge. *But at least her* stuff *can*.

Isn't that how we are sometimes? When pain hits us, we can't move on. It's like we're stuck in a cave. We need something to jar us free.

The grumpy old man's trip is meant to take him back, to a yesterday. He carries Ellie with him as much as he can—and by extension, to a happier time, when he felt more complete. But circumstances (and a young stowaway named Russell) push him out of his comfort zone and—with the help of Russell, a talking dog named Dug, and a bizarre, chocolate-loving bird named Kevin—he's forced to care about something in the here and now, and how to make sure his new friends survive it. Instead of being stuck in the past, he turns toward the future, to tomorrow, and finds that the sun really does rise over there.

Just like Ellie tried to tell him.

In a book they'd kept since they were kids, one Ellie labeled "Stuff I'm Going to Do," he finds Ellie's hopes and dreams—not of Paradise Falls, but of real, quieter adventures that she and Carl experienced together. Painting and holding hands and laughing with Carl while having a picnic. The book is filled with pictures. Memories. Treasured moments they shared, from weddings to road trips to quiet days at home.

Then, near the end, the pictures run out, and Carl turns the page—physically and, perhaps, metaphorically. And there he finds one last note from Ellie, hidden these many months because of Carl's pain and grief.

"Thanks for the adventure," it reads. "Now go have a new one!"

LEARNING TO FLY. AGAIN.

Some hurts never go away. When we lose someone close to us—a parent, a child, a spouse—do we ever really get over it? Don't we carry that hurt with us always? There's nothing anyone can say that makes us feel better. When someone suggests to us that there's reason behind it—that it's all part of God's plan—we sometimes want to scream. Maybe it's true. But it doesn't help. When a pain like that comes, nothing helps. Sometimes, when we're in that prison of hurt, we just need someone to sit with us. Listen to us cry or rage. Be there.

It'd be nice if God would take away the worst of our pain. I'd very much like that. But he doesn't. He lets us suffer. He lets us hurt.

But he is there. Even in the times we don't feel him, he's present. "Aren't two sparrows sold for a small coin?" Matthew tells us. "But not one of them will fall to the ground without your Father knowing about it already" (Matt. 10:29). It's a hard reality that they fall at all, but we can take a little comfort in the fact that they don't fall alone. He's with us. I believe he mourns with us, even. Jesus wept for his friends who were hurting. I don't think God acts any differently.

And yet as much as it hurts, we slowly find a way forward—just like Carl. There comes a time when we can smile again. Laugh. Take joy in the people around us. Carl finds a truth that Ellie wanted him to find. Life goes on. Life can still be precious and full of joy. That joy doesn't make everything magically better; Carl, I'm sure, still misses Ellie every day. But he found a way forward. He found a way to Tomorrow.

CHAPTER 7

THE ONE WHO KNOCKS

Television Antiheroes and the Evil in All of Us

You can look the other way once, and it's no big deal, except it makes it easier for you to compromise the next time, and pretty soon that's all you're doing: compromising, because that's the way you think things are done. You know those guys I busted? You think they were the bad guys? Because they weren't, they weren't bad guys, they were just like you and me. Except they compromised. . . . Once.

—Jack Bauer (Kiefer Sutherland), *24*

Y**ou know what's wrong with TV** these days? Casual Fridays.

Oh, they're fine in the real world. Great, in fact. Or so I've heard. My employer doesn't do casual Fridays (or casual any other day, either; they stopped mandating evening wear just a few years ago), but if they did, I'd go to work in my Superman footie pajamas. Or maybe a flannel shirt, swimming trunks, and an elegant prairie bonnet. Or perhaps I'd just paste a bunch of used sticky notes on my bod. Who knows? On casual Fridays, anything goes! I'd be ever so much more productive.

But on television, there's something comforting about your characters staying in uniform. Otherwise . . . chaos.

Now, follow me for a minute here. Back in television's earliest days, before the world came in color and when the Static Network dominated the rotary dial of television (their motto: "You can't miss our hiss!"), people watched a lot of Westerns. They were filled with all sorts of things that still make up the American West today: cows and horses and guns and drunks and old-timey piano players. But most especially, they were brimming with archetypal characters—good guys and bad guys. It didn't matter if you flicked on the channel halfway through the Western, because it was obvious who was who: the good guys shaved regularly, twirled their guns, treated the local ladies with self-effacing respect, and had a curious love of fringe. Sometimes they'd even grab a nearby guitar and burst into song. (Why? Have no clue. To chime in with the old-timey piano players, maybe?) The bad guys, meanwhile, would spit and sneer and quaff heavy liquor and looked like they bathed once a year—maybe not even that much if it was a drought year. And they'd never, under any circumstances, sing.

And (except for Hopalong Cassidy), the good guys almost always wore white hats, even after Labor Day. The villains wore basic black.

Those early Westerns taught us well. For decades, we often knew our heroes by what they wore. Was someone on television dressed as a police officer? Doctor? Priest? We'd count on them to do right by us. And even if shows tweaked the uniform a little, the hero still wore one. Yes, Boss Hogg on *The Dukes of Hazzard* wore nothing but white. But his sparkling suit made him all the more recognizable (and the story was more rewarding when he fell in the mud). Sure, *Dallas*'s J. R. Ewing had a few white hats in his closet. But the cowboy hat—in all its wide-brimmed, ten-gallon glory—was his signature look. His uniform, if you will. He might as well have had a nametag on his chest labeled *J. R. Ewing, Villain* and greeted everyone who came through Southfork's doors with a drawling, "Hi! How can I ruin your life today?" We recognized our television characters, both good and bad, the same way we'd recognize a fast-food attendant or a banker or a bellboy: by what they wore.

But then came casual Friday, and everything went haywire. Not only did everyone start wearing jeans and flip-flops to work, but our television characters dropped their signature uniforms too. We couldn't tell a good guy by his job anymore. Heck, sometimes today, you don't even know who the good guys *are* anymore. Why, a Los Angeles detective could be a crooked, no-good louse who still catches bad guys (*The Shield*). A brilliant surgeon might be a world-class jerk (*House*). A mob boss might be a doting family man (*The Sopranos*). A Miami forensics consultant might be a strangely ethical serial killer (*Dexter*). How are we supposed to know who to root for these days? How can we tell the good guys from the bad?

We're in the age of the antihero now, where every good guy has a skeleton or twenty in their closet, every bad guy has a sickly mother he's trying to help, and traditional white-hatted heroes have gone the way of the Pony Express. The character of television is so twisted now that it looks like . . . well, like real life.

We like to think of ourselves as the heroes of our own stories—characters who wear the white hats. But the truth is a little more complex. Sometimes we lie or cheat or behave dishonorably. Sometimes, if we're honest with ourselves, our actions don't match up with the fringe-sporting cowboys of yesteryear.

That's the unavoidable reality of living in a fallen world. We kinda suck. No wonder we like our antiheroes so much.

TICK, TOCK, TICK, TOCK. . .

The 2014 miniseries *24: Live Another Day* marked the return of Keifer Sutherland's Jack Bauer, one of television's most iconic, most tortured, most psychopathic heroes. In a television landscape filled with bad-boy do-gooders, he was one of the first, one of the best . . . and one of the baddest.

From the time *24* debuted in the fall of 2001 (just a couple months after 9/11), the show has always been about just how far Jack will go to get the bad guys and save the world. Answer? As far as he needs to. He ripped out someone's jugular with his teeth. He chopped off his own partner's hand. He killed his own boss. (That'll look bad on the annual job review, I'd imagine.) Jack's so hardcore, he can threaten someone with a *towel*.

"You probably don't think that I can force this towel down your throat," he growls in Day 1 (that'd be season 1, for you *24* neophytes). "But trust me, I can. All the way."

Jack Bauer is the MacGyver of torture. He makes Chuck Norris look like a footman from *Downton Abbey*.

Over *24*'s eight-season run (and one made-for-television movie), Jack has killed anywhere from 266 to 270 people, according to the (always reliable) Internet, and that's not counting the folks he offed in *Live Another Day*. Keep in mind that *24* always focuses on one chronological day, so that means Jack's killed nearly three hundred folks in about *eight days*.

But for all that death and mayhem, Jack is still the good guy. He saves the world at least once every season. And what thanks does he get? Zilch. Jack has lost everything in his quest to keep America safe: his wife, his friends, his job (several times), his freedom, his health, and maybe a good chunk of his sanity. He's stared death in the eye more often than the dude from *Groundhog Day*. And strangely, he became something of a cult hero to evangelical Christians—never mind the fact that the only time he mentions God or Jesus is when he's cursing.

Back in 2010, Stephanie Drury even listed Jack Bauer on her blog list of "Stuff Christian Culture Likes." "He's macho, tenacious and tech-savvy (all qualities that Christian culture holds dear) and he's working his a— off under an apocalyptic deadline, which Christians can relate to."

Part of the evangelical affection for Jack probably can be attributed to politics. Mr. Bauer and conservative Christianity seem to share a certain affection for Dick Cheney. But Jack also is a courageous, self-sacrificing hero, willing to put himself on the line for the sake of others. And that resonates deeply with our own spiritual story. Jack Bauer suffers for our sake. He sacrifices himself to save the world. You could argue the guy could be something of a Christlike figure . . . if Jesus were prone to shooting Pharisees in the kneecaps.

"In the early years of *24*, after the 9/11 attacks, the common take was that the appeal of Jack Bauer lay in his strength," writes *Time*'s James Poniewozik.

> He was tough, decisive, and effective, offering the fantasy of security in an insecure time. But in the long run,

I don't think Bauer's most important function was to fight our battles; it was to feel our pain. Season after season, he would suffer physically and spiritually, he would lose friends and lovers (and sleep), he would save the country and get run out of town. He was like a psychic pincushion, a sponge soaking up all the toxic emotion of the era, committing our sins and swallowing the guilt until he seemed 100 years old.

It's interesting the language Poniewozik uses, words like *sin* and *guilt*. Jack does, in his own deeply warped way, echo our faith. If he had a Bible verse stitched on a throw pillow, it'd come from one of those angry psalms that talk about enemies being food for jackals. Maybe something like Psalm 68:21-23:

> *Yes, God will shatter the heads of his enemies—*
> *the very skulls of those who walk in guilt.*
> *My Lord has spoken:*
> *"From Bashan I will bring those people back.*
> *I will bring them back from the ocean's depths*
> *so that you can wash your feet in their blood,*
> *   so that your dogs' tongues*
> *   can lap up their share of your enemies."*

Those angry psalms talk about God punishing the "violent men" surrounding the psalmist, and they speak in a language that Jack surely would appreciate.

But Jack himself is a violent man, and he knows it. He's done horrible things. While Jesus, sinless, wiped clean our sins, Jack sins so that we don't have to. He, as Poniewozik says, swallows our guilt. Jack is a savior in a world without grace, a hero damned to his own eternal hell. In *24*, the wages of sin are indeed death. And Jack Bauer, our secular angel of death, is himself one of the walking dead: a zombie who has turned his back on any normal, rational life to do what he feels he must. He cannot rest in peace. He cannot rest at all.

As he says in the first hour of *Live Another Day*, "There's no going back for me."

UNDER OUR OWN POWER

When you look at our legion of antiheroes, a curious thread seems to run through many of them: they are people who have taken it upon themselves to fix the world, to remake it—or their little corner of it—into something more pleasing to them, more perfect. Maybe they, like Jack, want to make the world a better place. Maybe they just want to find some beauty in this ugly world, some goodness in a bad universe. But without help, particularly the help of God, they're bound to screw it up. Just like we are.

Consider: Tony Soprano (James Gandolfini) in HBO's *The Sopranos* struggles to do right by the people he loves. And in the show's six seasons (1999–2007), we've seen that love manifested in touching but often conflicted ways. Yes, he may be a father who wants to do everything he can for his kids. He may be a husband who wants to better care for his wife. But his own volcanic temper and serial philandering get in the way—not to mention his career as a mafia boss.

Carmela (Mrs. Soprano to you) has always wanted husband Tony to inch closer to the light: "My priest said I should work with him, help him to become a better man," she tells psychiatrist Dr. Krakower in the third season.

"How's that going?" Dr. Krakower asks.

However, Krakower already knows the answer. People like Tony don't change. Not without help. But Tony answers to no authority but his own, trusts in no power but his guns and his goons. He may kneel on occasion to God's throne, but he hardly believes someone's actually sitting there.

Consider: Philip and Elizabeth (Matthew Rhys and Keri Russell) in FX's *The Americans* (2013–present), a seemingly normal 1980s-era suburban couple who are also Soviet spies, doing their best to topple our corrupt capitalist regime. They're the mirror image of Jack Bauer in a way, only with less red-eye, more Red. Both believe in the cause, especially Elizabeth. Both will do whatever they must to help Mother Russia: lie, have sex with an American government worker bee, kill.

But they're human too. Their children, teenager Paige and tween Henry, have no idea what their parents actually do for a living, and Philip and Elizabeth fear for their safety. Their upscale surroundings are so much better than what they'd find in Moscow, and Philip particularly finds the American lifestyle tempting. They must make some pretty cataclysmic moral compromises. And the world, which seemed so obvious and clear when Philip and Elizabeth were in spy camp or whatever, is getting muddier. They, like all good antiheroes, must puzzle out what's black and white in a slate-gray world. They have no God to turn to for help, no faith from which to seek guidance. And that's a problem.

In a 2014 episode, Henry is caught breaking into a neighbor's house to play video games. When Philip and Elizabeth confront him, he bursts into tears. "I know the difference between right and wrong. . . . You know that!" he wails. "I'm good, I am! I'm a good person . . . !"

Henry echoes almost every character on *The Americans*. They believe they're good. They know they've done wrong, but they insist it's for the right reasons. And yet when we watch them, what they say and do, we see the conflict in them. The hypocrisy. Their actions expose the gray within them all.

Consider: Dexter (Michael C. Hall) from Showtime's long-running drama of the same name (2006–2013). The guy has a prototypical "white hat" job—that of a forensics expert for the Miami police force. But he was, for years, also a serial killer. He has suffered from schizoid personality disorder from childhood, unable to love or mourn or even *feel* much of anything, like the friends and family around him. He has no conscience to speak of, but from an early age, Dexter was taught and even encouraged to sate his horrific compulsion—his unquenchable thirst to kill—on only those who deserved it.

Dexter believed that his work was, in its own terrible way, good. He's an atheist, after all, and Dexter believes the only true judgment these dark souls can expect is by Dexter's own bloody hands.

Dexter killed around 135 people in his bloody Showtime reign (fewer than Jack Bauer, of course, but not many people have Jack's manic endurance). And yet, of all the characters we've talked about here, our atheist serial killer Dexter has had the most flirtations with faith. Indeed, in season 6, spirituality becomes a prime focus of the show.

Despite his lack of belief, Dexter wonders whether he should raise his son, Harrison, as a Christian, hoping to have something better to pass on to him than a disturbing set of murder genes. And when his son gets sick, he even prays at one point, begging God to save him. Most critically, Dexter meets a guy called Brother Sam—a former killer who, through what Sam considers divine intervention, was rescued from death row. He now serves God from the bowels of his own body shop, employing other ex-cons while trying to point them in a better direction. He does what he can to help Dexter too. Even after Sam is shot and lies dying in the hospital, he pleads with Dexter to forgive the assailant, Nick, leading to one of the most poignant exchanges in the series.

"You don't know me," Dexter says, looking over the dying Sam.

"Yes, I do," Sam says. "I know about your darkness, but I also see your light."

"If there's light in me I don't feel it," Dexter tells him. "I just want to hurt Nick. You don't know how much I wanna hurt him."

"You need to forgive him," Sam says.

"I don't know how."

"Just let it go," Sam says. "You can't live with hate in your heart. It'll eat you up inside. You gotta find some peace in life."

"Nick doesn't deserve it."

"It ain't about him, Dexter. If you don't let that darkness go, it won't let go of you. Let it go, let it go."

Now, before you start singing that song from *Frozen*, let's think about what Sam says here. He asks Dexter to *forgive*. Even as death approaches, Sam's eyes are fixed on God. He's trying to show Dexter a better way to live. It's both an echo of Jesus' own last words on the cross and a realistic look at how we all must try to move on from life's bitterest moments.

When we are hurt by someone, or when someone hurts a person we love, we want, like Dexter, to make that person suffer. We want vengeance. It's a very normal, very human reaction—and strangely in this context, a sign that perhaps Brother Sam's tutelage has helped Dex find a shred of human emotion under his pathological skin. And yet, he wants Dexter to look for something even better—to find the better angels of his nature, rather than always the angel of death.

Dexter does not, of course. He defies Brother Sam's last request and drowns Nick in the surf—in the very same water in which Brother Sam had once, in better times, baptized Nick.

REAPING THE WHIRLWIND

Our antiheroes rarely find happy endings.

In *Dexter*'s series finale, Showtime's favorite serial killer loses perhaps the only two people he ever loved, killing one and deserting the other (both, it's suggested, for their own good). He walks away, utterly alone.

In the final episode of *The Sopranos*, we see Tony, Carmela, and son A. J. eating onion rings in a restaurant, the Journey song "Don't Stop Believing" playing in the background. A nervous-looking man heads to the restroom. Two other toughs walk in. And then, just as Tony looks to the front door and Journey's Steve Perry sings, "Don't stop," the screen goes black. Darkness envelops the family, just as Tony's own darkness permeated the show from the first episode to the last.

We can't say what will happen with Philip and Elizabeth from *The Americans*. Perhaps Jack Bauer's story isn't done, either. But television is often just as cruel as Jack, as wrathful as an Old Testament prophet. "There will be no mercy in judgment for anyone who hasn't shown mercy," we read in James 2:13. "As I've observed, those who plow sin / and sow trouble will harvest it," says Job 4:8. As *we* have seen, these characters did not find mercy. They have not asked for grace or forgiveness. And so they found none.

"I'm good!" Henry told us in *The Americans*. "I'm a good person!" We all say the same. But it's our actions that tell the truth of the matter, our deeds that suggest who or what we follow. Temptations have a way of short-circuiting our good intentions. We sometimes compromise for what seem like the best of reasons. But those compromises, those lapses in judgment, often come back to bite us in the rear. And there's perhaps no better example of that than Walter White.

BREAKING

Walter White (Bryan Cranston), in AMC's great-but-graphic *Breaking Bad* (2008–2013), would've again been a prototypical white-hat guy: a dutiful husband, the father of a special-needs son, a mostly good man. He was a teacher, for cryin' out loud, and anyone brave enough to teach chemistry in high school is a better man than me. Even his name sounds nice: Walter White. Would a *Walter* ever do anything bad?

However, Walt also has inoperable lung cancer, and you can't battle cancer on a teacher's salary. Apparently not in New Mexico, at least.

But Walt runs into Jesse Pinkman (Aaron Paul), former student, current drug dealer, and all-around punk. And before the pilot episode's done, they form a wacky partnership cooking methamphetamine. It makes perfect sense, really: Walt's got the chemistry background to brew up the best meth this side of Alabama. Jesse has the connections to distribute. With all due apologies to Casablanca, it's the beginning of a not-so-beautiful relationship—a relationship that lasted five seasons.

But it almost didn't last five shows.

In the program's fifth episode, "Gray Matter," Walt has turned his back on Jesse and meth and plans to just let the stage 3 cancer run its course. Better to die than to sell your soul, he figures. But when a former colleague offers to pay for Walt's treatment, Walt refuses that too. He tells his wife, Skyler, that he wants to sleep in his own bed, keep his hair, enjoy whatever is left of his life.

"That is my thought process, Skyler," he says. "I choose not to do it."

When he sees how much fighting the disease means to his wife, though, he reluctantly agrees. But instead of accepting help from his old friend, he turns once again to Jesse. The episode ends with Walt, nearly in tears, standing before his once-and-future partner. "Wanna cook?" he says.

We know the trajectory of Walter's life from there. Oh, he still thinks he's a good person—or, at least, that he's cooking for good reasons. He cooks to pay for treatment. To provide for his family. To satisfy debts and fulfill promises. He, like Henry from *The Americans*, would say he knows right from wrong. He rationalizes his actions, excuses the murders he commits. And bit by bit, the good guy that was Walter White disappears into his alter ego, Heisenberg. In Goethe, Faust sells his soul with the stroke of a pen; White sells his an ounce at a time.

We knew where Walt would wind up, of course. His fate was given away the minute we saw the title screen. Walter White broke bad an episode at a time, rationalizing all the way. It isn't until the very end that he admits the truth.

"I did it for me," he tells Skyler. "I liked it. I was good at it. And, I was really . . . I was alive."

The first step toward forgiveness is confession, and Walt takes that step with this statement. "With this line, it's almost as if Walt completes his journey from Mr. Chips to Scarface and then moves back a little bit toward the good man that he once was," writes Aaron Couch of *The Hollywood Reporter*. He has no opportunity for penance; he has no time left. But he does what he can to protect his wife and children before accepting his own bloody end.

It was the end that he deserved in a television world without grace. Without forgiveness. And yet in that fifth episode, a hand was offered to him. Help was extended. Through his former colleague, Walt was given a second chance. And he chose to turn away. He chose to try to save himself.

HEALING THE BROKEN, BETTERING THE BAD

It never seems to work, looking for salvation through our own strength. The Golden Age of Television Antiheroes tells us the same thing that the Bible has for thousands of years: we can't save ourselves. We have to be willing to change. And we need help to do it.

After all, we're not much better than Walt. Not really. We may not be meth cookers or serial killers or Soviet spies, but we're all sinners. We can be jerks sometimes. Selfish. We lie and cheat. We may think of ourselves as good people, but if we were judged on what we did when no one was looking, well, not very many of us would have a great case in court. But we can lean on something else, you and I. God's love and grace.

"You are saved by God's grace because of your faith," Paul says in Ephesians 2:8-9. "This salvation is God's gift. It's not something you possessed. It's not something you did that you can be proud of."

Like Brother Sam, we know we're sinners. Like Brother Sam, we know there's nothing we can do about it. But instead of trying to work our way toward salvation or giving up and walking the world like Jack Bauer, angry and damned, we ask for forgiveness.

And here's the beautiful thing: we get it.

CHAPTER 8
WELL, *THAT'S* DIFFERENT

Christians and the Weird World of Reality Television

Do we look like beauty contestants to you?
—Si Robertson, *Duck Dynasty*

S ay the words *reality television,* and even atheists will tell you they're a sign of the end times. Surely one of those sealed scrolls had something to say about those poor Kardashians.

And sometimes, it's hard to argue. It has spawned such horrors as *Bridalplasty* and *Amish Mafia* and has given the Jersey Shore a bad name. If pop culture was a family reunion, reality television would be your loud cousin from Vegas—the one with the rhinestone shirt and the cowboy boots made of panda leather. If pop culture's an orchestra, reality television is the electric kazoo.

No one admits to watching reality television. Not you, not me, no one. Even the cast of *The Real Housewives of Atlanta* insist they watch nothing but *Downton Abbey.* You'd think the whole genre would've fallen over like a badly constructed wedding cake, smushed underneath the weight of its own shame. But according to Nielsen, *somebody's* watching this stuff. ABC's *Dancing with the Stars*, in its nineteenth season (as of this writing), is still getting more than twelve million viewers a week. That's nearly as many as the number of viewers who watch prestige dramas such as *Mad Men, Game of Thrones, The Americans, Homeland,* and *House of Cards* . . . combined.

But despite its reputation, reality television isn't all bad. In fact, some of it is actually pretty watchable. Good, even.

Or so I've heard.

(Awkward pause.)

And when it comes to spreading the good news, reality TV can even be kinda great. There's no other genre in which out-and-proud Christians are so visible, so popular, or, in some cases, so hairy.

COME AND LISTEN TO A STORY 'BOUT A MAN NAMED SI . . .

If you want to blame someone for reality television's bad reputation, you could do worse than point at A&E. Around 2003, the network (then known as the Arts & Entertainment Network) began chucking more highbrow and scripted fare out the screen door in favor of cheaper, slimier reality shows such as *Dog the Bounty Hunter* and *Gene Simmons Family Jewels.* The network was, in some respects, a prime purveyor of exploitation television, encouraging viewers to laugh at someone's ludicrous antics (see *Gene Simmons* above) or gape in abject, voyeuristic horror at their serious problems (*Intervention, Hoarders*). The network once known for bringing lit-based dramas such as *Emma* and *The Mayor of Casterbridge* to small screens in the United States was now a reality television freak show, according to critics—and the freakier the family, the better.

No wonder they were interested in the Robertsons.

The family had built a thriving business predicated on manufacturing duck calls. The men looked like bearded hillbillies, and perhaps they were—backwoods enthusiasts that had struck it rich but still liked wading around in the Louisiana muck, shooting anything that moved. They were like *The Beverly Hillbillies*, only with more facial hair. Probably no one at A&E's New York headquarters knew families like this ever existed. The Robertsons, after all, lived in quintessential flyover country—strange, bizarre lands completely lacking such basic necessities as sushi bars and overpriced lattes.

Maybe some A&E execs knew the Robertsons were, for all their facial hair, surprisingly sophisticated businessmen and savvy entertainers (they'd been selling videos of their hunting and fishing trips to customers for years). But I imagine others looked at the Robertsons and thought, *They'll fit right into our freak show.*

But when *Duck Dynasty* hit American homes, something kinda weird happened. Not only did folks watch because the Robertsons were so different; they watched because they felt strangely familiar. Forget *Keeping Up with the Kardashians* or *The Real Housewives of Beverly Hills* or any slew of programs that chronicled exotic lives completely foreign to most of our experiences. Sure, the Robertsons were different than we were—way different, in many cases. But they were strangely similar too. They cared for one another. They played jokes on one another. They got on one another's nerves. And before the episode ended, they'd all gather 'round the family table for dinner, and then . . . pray.

Crazy, huh? Not many other families on television, whether they're on sitcoms, dramas, or reality television, pray. America is overwhelmingly Christian still, but you'd never know it from our TV shows . . . except for *Duck Dynasty*.

For a while, some folks at A&E didn't like where the show was going. According to an interview that dour patriarch Phil Robertson gave to the Christian magazine *Sports Spectrum*, the show's editors occasionally "bleeped" profanity that wasn't actually there (an attempt to make the Robertsons sound edgier, I guess) and always chopped off the name *Jesus* in the Robertsons' traditional prayer. Phil pushed back on both practices, bringing up for the latter that our whole calendar is set around the birth of Jesus. "You Hollywood cats are counting time by Jesus just like I am," he said, adding, "I don't think it would hurt to throw his name in there time to time."

Duck Dynasty became the biggest hit in A&E history and the most popular nonscripted (using the term loosely) cable show ever. But it hasn't all been sun and daisies for the family.

The Robertsons ran into a public relations buzzsaw after Phil Robertson made some rather unfortunate, very public, and, in my opinion, pretty embarrassing comments about homosexuality and slavery in *GQ* magazine.

It wasn't the first time Phil had caused problems. The family nearly unraveled because of him long before *Duck Dynasty*. According to Phil's wife, "Miss Kay," their marriage was incredibly strained for a while. Phil was drinking a lot and cheating. Kay actually took her boys and left for a while. "It got about as bad as it can get," Kay confessed to *Us* magazine. She told her boys that the devil had ahold of Phil, asking them to hate Satan, not their father. She even considered killing herself.

Kay never stopped fighting for their relationship, and when Phil rediscovered Christianity, he began to turn his life around. But it was only the first step. In a 2014 interview with the *Christian Post*'s Allison Takeda, Kay recalled her son Jason asking whether the devil was leaving Phil since Jesus had taken up residence. "I said, 'Yes, Jesus is living in your dad, but still he's going to have a lot of help, because he doesn't know how to be good. And so we have to help teach him how to be good.'"

Phil and the rest of the family are still learning how to be good, I think—learning, just like the rest of us are.

The Robertsons aren't perfect. They've had their struggles. They'll have some in the future too. And let me be honest, when I heard Phil's controversial *GQ* statements, I cringed. Maybe some of you did as well. Others might've sighed at the extraordinary secular blowback, viewing it as a politically correct firestorm that nearly got Phil booted from his own show and spelled the end of a little bit of television magic.

But that's a sobering and, in some ways, beautiful illustration of what Christianity is: a huge, extended family full of very different people. The Christian family is, frankly, a lot like the Robertson family. We can exasperate each other. We can disagree with each other. And some of our Christian brothers and sisters can seem a little crazy at times—a little like the Robertsons' Uncle Si (without his penchant for feather boas).

But when dinnertime comes, I like to think that we Christians—Catholic and Orthodox and Protestant, mainline and evangelical, liberal and conservative—join hands at the same table, bow our heads, and pray to the same God to which we agree we owe everything. I'd like to think that, in spite of our quirky habits and serious differences, we love each other still.

FLIPPING ON FAITH

As I mentioned earlier, faith is often ignored on television, particularly scripted television. And when a show *does* decide to broach this controversial topic, it often does so through tokenism: a sole Christian character serves as a foil through which to examine an issue with a spiritual component—to press an atheist, perhaps, or to reflect on the possibility of deeper truth or some such. Even when a Christian character somehow lands as a regular on a show, the character's Christianity becomes the character's only real defining characteristic—an attitude that NBC's mega-meta show *Community* slyly ribs with its own token Christian, Shirley, who sometimes throws "pool parties" to secretly baptize her friends. ("Well, excuse me for trying to sneak you into heaven!" she huffs.)

But reality television—perhaps because it's theoretically more "real" and all (*Amish Mafia* notwithstanding)—seems to have a few more job openings for Christians.

Sometimes that too smacks of tokenism. Casting directors can't help it. When a show's whole point is to see what happens when you throw outlandishly different people together—say, a pot-smoking lesbian rodeo clown with a Satan-worshiping paraplegic accountant—well, why not throw a conservative Christian in the mix too? That's television gold right there.

That sort of stunt casting began in reality television's infancy, and Christians were a part of the mix from the get-go. The grand-pappy of all modern reality TV shows, MTV's *The Real World*, snagged conservative Christian Jon Brennan for its second season in 1993 (*The Real World: Los Angeles.*) In a show predicated on shoving scads of divergent people under the same roof to see what happens, Jon seemed just about perfect. He wore a big cowboy hat, didn't drink, loved Jesus, and was (gasp) a virgin. He was eighteen then—younger than anyone else in the house—but that didn't keep him from speaking his mind. A lot.

Maybe today, a guy like that'd be run out of the house quicker than a conservative Mozilla CEO, but in 1993, MTV just let the cameras roll. And before the season was through, Jon became one of *The Real World*'s most real people. Sure, he endured more than his fair share of ribbing, but Jon cobbled together some strong friendships on the show. And when another housemate, Tami, got pregnant and had an abortion (one of the few times any television show has dealt with the issue), Jon showed deep compassion while still holding firm to his stance that abortion is wrong.

The Real World will never be on anyone's short list as an evangelistic tool. But for those who watched, Jon showed a secular world a Christian both stereotypical and disarmingly real. He became one of the season's most popular characters and, perhaps for a few, offered a winsome window into a faith they'd not seriously considered before.

Many Christians following in Jon's boot steps have found opportunities to speak up for themselves and their God on reality television.

In 2003, on the first season of *America's Next Top Model*, Christian contestants Shannon Stewart and Robin Manning both refused to pose in the buff in the seventh episode. (Robin was punished the most severely for the decision and was promptly voted out, while Shannon held on for a couple more episodes and was named the runner-up.)

In the fifth season of *American Idol*—a show that has long given audiences a steady stream of Christian singers who polished their singing chops at church—a contestant named Mandisa became the target for some harsh, weight-focused jibes by notoriously jagged-tongued judge Simon Cowell. When she finished her audition, Cowell wondered whether *American Idol* would need "a bigger stage." And when fellow judge Paula Abdul said that Mandisa was "like Frenchie," a previous contestant, Cowell said, "Forget Frenchie, she's like France."

Mandisa came back later to confront Cowell, but in the best way possible. "What I want to say to you is that, yes, you hurt me and I cried, and it was painful. It really was," she began. "But I want you to know that I've forgiven you. And that you don't need someone to apologize in order to forgive somebody. And I figure that if Jesus could die so that all of my wrongs could be forgiven, then I can certainly extend that same grace to you." She went onto make the show's Top 9, and, while she didn't win the season, she's become a major force in Christian music and has released (as of 2014) four studio albums. The first was named, appropriately, *True Beauty*.

Sean Lowe became the seventeenth paramour for ABC's *The Bachelor* in 2013—a show predicated on him sorting through and frequently smooching more than two dozen women to find, supposedly, the One. But Lowe was also an evangelical Christian—one who had been celibate for six years. So just how is a sex-abstaining Christian supposed to navigate a show that boasts scads of gorgeous (and obviously *very* available) women and a camera-free Fantasy Suite? "It's unnatural to date twenty-five women at one time," he admitted on the Christian site *I Am Second.* "And it felt wrong. A lot of the time it felt wrong."

But Lowe didn't sleep with anyone on the show, and he survived the rose-toting gauntlet just fine. In the season's final episode, he proposed to Catherine Giudici. They got hitched on January 26, 2014—the first bachelor in the series's seventeen seasons to actually marry the person to whom he proposed on the show. Both said they planned to remain celibate until their wedding night. Shortly before their wedding, Jimmy Kimmel hooked them both to lie detectors and had a professional polygraph expert ask if they'd slept together. According to the polygraph, they had kept their vow before they said their vows.

"I have to say, I'm proud and disappointed at the same time," Kimmel said.

DARE TO BE DIFFERENT

There are more examples we could give. Dozens, maybe. Hundreds. We don't have that sort of space, of course, but even with this small sample size we see an interesting trend emerge. These

Christians we see on reality TV are *different*. They go against the grain, stand out from their fellow contestants, and sometimes shock talk-show hosts.

The fact that they're different helped get them drafted into the world of reality television in the first place, of course; unless the show has something to do with cloning, no casting director wants to stock a show with sixteen contestants who all look and act the same. That's just bad television. They *want* people to stand out. They *want* color. And in a society where even your Aunt Edna is angling for a reality show and pop starlets have to resort to wearing a meat dress to get attention (Lady Gaga) or, better yet, wear nothing at all, Christians who don't take off their clothes—Christians who actually practice what they preach—are about as colorful and as different as it gets.

And that's altogether fitting, really. We Christians are supposed to be different. We're not supposed to be like everybody else.

"Don't be conformed to the patterns of this world, but be transformed by the renewing of your minds so that you can figure out what God's will is—what is good and pleasing and mature," Paul writes in Romans 12:2. Back in his day, Christians were wildly different from the Romans around them, of course—a tiny, strange cult that made the rest of society pretty nervous. And no wonder: most Romans didn't know much about Christianity, other than that their most sacred rite had something to do with eating someone's body and drinking his blood. No wonder they were treated with a little suspicion.

But once that little misunderstanding was cleared up, Romans began to be attracted by Christian differences—their love, their capacity to forgive, and all the rest. Even their strict morality was attractive. Truth is, unbridled hedonism can get pretty exhausting after a while.

And Christians, even though they technically make up nearly 80 percent of the US population, still feel different. Those who walk the walk, anyway. While lots of us call ourselves Christians, sometimes we don't act like it very much. We might think about going to church sometimes, but that doesn't keep us from lying or getting drunk or sleeping with our not-so-significant others. Yeah, it's easy to call yourself a Christian. But to let the faith change your life? That's tough stuff.

When we see someone on television actually act like a Christian, it feels weird. Countercultural. "Man, those folks are odd," some might say while watching the Robertsons on *Duck Dynasty* or the latest Christian on *Survivor*. But maybe some say it with a hint of curiosity. Maybe they think they're odd in a good way. And perhaps they begin to wonder whether those odd Christians know something that they do not.

"I don't know if anyone's found Jesus through me talking about not having sex," Sean Lowe said in his *I Am Second* testimony. "But I think it's now certainly more evident than ever that I love Jesus, and that I'm different because I love Jesus."

Shouldn't we all be a little different?

REAL PROBLEMS TOO

'Course, *different* isn't automatically *good*. Some Christians who have appeared on reality television have come across as judgmental jerks. Every character we've talked about so far has had their share of detractors (except Mandisa, 'cause everybody loves Mandisa). And because reality shows are specifically designed to make contestants feel uncomfortable, Christian contestants can be forced into really awkward and apparently hypocritical positions. For instance, her fellow contestants on *America's Next Top Model* wondered why Robin was so upset at the thought of posing nude when she was just fine shaking her womanly wiles. You might even wonder whether competing in such a contest is compatible with the Christian walk at all. For every Christian who says that we should be proud of the bodies God gave us (being made in his image, and all), there might be two or three who wonder whether we should be quite *that* proud—or trigger quite so much temptation among some of those watching. Lowe, from *The Bachelor*, had the same sort of question running through his mind.

"What if I'm harming my testimony by going on a show and dating multiple people at one time, and kissing multiple people?" Lowe asked himself. "What if people look at me and they say, 'This is what is wrong with Christianity'? Look at this guy. He's professing one thing, and going on TV and doing the opposite. That was a big fear."

And even when Christians do everything right, there's no guarantee that that's what the viewing audience sees at home. TV execs and producers aren't there to spread the good news. They're there to make good TV—or, if that's not possible, bad TV that people want to watch. In order to draw in viewers, you've got to have compelling reasons for them to tune in. You must have drama. Conflict. Scandal. And if there's some skin, so much the better.

All that helps explain why we're seeing more and more uncomfortably Christian reality shows pop up: Discovery Channel's bizarre *Amish Mafia*, for instance—a show that resembles the Amish people about as much as FX's *The Americans* resembles most Americans. Or there's National Geographic's *Snake Salvation*, an examination of the snake-handling Pentecostals that represent about one one-millionth of Christianity's worldwide breadth.

"Network producers and executives aren't really interested in the 'hilarious antics' of your pastor and his family," Christian producer Phil Cooke told the Religion News Service in 2013. "They're more interested in seeing the pastor lose his temper in a staff meeting, toss his mobile phone against the wall, and storm out of the room. Like it or not, it's conflict that drives most reality programming."

Let's face it: while good Christians may stand out on a secular reality program, a show built on good Christian behavior is about as thrilling as a zoo made up of vegetarian boa constrictors. Yeah, watching a snake swallow a cantaloupe would be awesome . . . once. But it seems like the novelty might wear thin after a while.

Or would it?

ARE YOU SMARTER THAN AN AMORITE?

For three years, the Game Show Network has been trotting out metaphorical vegetarian boa constrictors—well-meaning people of faith who compete for sorta big money on the *American Bible*

Challenge. And viewers just—well, eat it up. The *Challenge* has been the network's highest-rated show for three straight years, surprising pert' near everyone—including host Jeff Foxworthy. He often hears from non-Christians who watch the show. "Well, I don't really go to church," they tell him, "but I kinda like that *Bible Challenge* show you do."

Foxworthy, a longtime comedian, part-time game show host, and a Christian since the age of seven, wasn't so sure he wanted to host another game show after his hit *Are You Smarter than a 5th Grader?* ended its three-year run on Fox.

"When I came back, I said, 'I'll do it if people don't keep the money,'" he told me in an interview. "The only people Jesus got sideways with were the Pharisees that had all this head knowledge but they had no heart knowledge. If these people are giving the money away and loving on somebody else, that's heart knowledge.'"

Every season, faith-based teams from across the country distribute some heart knowledge to viewers, all while displaying their head knowledge of the Bible. They're as divergent as can be: one week, a trio of nuns might face off against a team of Christian tattoo artists. The next, maybe it's a clutch of fresh-faced youth workers battling a faith-based basketball squad filled with octogenarians. Watching a few episodes of *American Bible Challenge* gives you a whole new appreciation of the Christian faith's dazzling breadth and bewildering diversity. "If you're on the outside looking in and you had a preconceived notion of what you thought a Christian looked like, you turn on our show and you think, *Well, I was wrong about that*," Foxworthy says.

And each team plays for charity. Some teams *are* the charity: whatever they win will be funneled back into the community in which they serve. And that, Foxworthy says, makes *American Bible Challenge* special—different in the best of ways from any other game show out there.

Just how different? Foxworthy found out in the first season, when Minnie's Food Pantry from Plano, Texas, took part in the show. The three women on the team had, for years, helped the community's hungry—sometimes with money out of their own pockets—feeding folks right through their back door. When they won the week's competition and the $20,000 that went along with it, Foxworthy saw that one of the women was sobbing.

"I went over there and I put my arm around her and I said, 'Are you OK?'" Foxworthy recalls. "And she said, 'Do you know what this means? This is 80,000 meals for people that weren't going to eat.' I was like, *oh, wow*. On any other game show, somebody would be buying a new motorcycle with that, or a boat. . . . This is different. This is cool."

To be a Christian, if you take being Christian seriously, means to be a little different. Your vision's a little clearer (we hope), your priorities a little tweaked. You deny yourself sometimes. You do your best to resist the temptations that come along. And maybe, in time, you find that you're growing stronger in your will, clearer in your convictions. It's not easy; no one ever said it was. I still struggle with this stuff every day. But I believe that, to be a Christian, you care for others more than you care for yourself. You follow in Jesus' footsteps as best as you can.

Those sorts of differences aren't seen much on television. But when they are, viewers notice. They glimpse, through the occasional game show contestant or reality program personality, something of the hands and feet of God. And maybe they see that Christianity can be meaningful. It can bring joy and peace. And most important, it can make the world a better place.

Perhaps they see that being different can make a difference.

CHAPTER 9
A JOYFUL NOISE

When It Comes to Faith, Music Is Noteworthy

I can't change the world
But I can change the world in me.
—U2, "Rejoice," from the album *October*

I n the spring of 2014, a bespectacled nun in sensible shoes walked onto the stage of Italy's version of *The Voice*, a ratings also-ran in need of a spark. The judges never saw her coming; the show requires that they sit with their back to contestants until they hear something special. Maybe the audience snickered a bit as they saw the woman walk onstage. A twenty-five-year-old nun in full habit, after all, would hardly seem the ideal candidate to become Europe's next big pop star.

Then Sister Cristina Scuccia began to sing.

Belting out Alicia Keys' song "No One," Sister Cristina brought the house to its feet in two seconds. One by one, the judges spun their chairs around to see just where this big, beautiful, blast-you-to-the-back-wall voice was coming from. They gasped when they saw the nun dancing and swaying on stage. Judge J-Ax, a rapper with a scruffy goatee and ink on his neck, fought back tears.

Before you could say "Susan Boyle," a star was born, and not just in Italy (though *The Voice*'s ratings shot up dramatically after the nun's appearance). A clip of Sister Cristina's opening performance was viewed more than fifty million times on YouTube, and her follow-up performances have netted millions more. For a while in 2014, she was pop culture's "It Girl."

But audiences enraptured by Sister Cristina's singing might've, in all the hubbub, missed who she was singing to. "No One," in which a girl declares her lifelong devotion to her beau no matter what the world might throw at them, took on a new meaning when belted out by a young woman who, in Catholic thought, had forsaken worldly romantic love to marry Jesus.

> So till the end of time I'm telling you there ain't no one No
>   one, no one
> Can get in the way of what I feel for you

"There is a tendency for music to need to be transgressive," the Reverend Raffaele Giacopuzzi, artistic director of the Christian-based Good News Festival and the person who unofficially discovered Sister Cristina, told the *New York Times*. "But today faith is the last transgression."

THE KEY OF BELIEF

If stories can be a path to the divine, songs are more like a *Star Trek* transporter. Music bypasses pesky rules of plot and logic and hops right to the heart. I don't know why, but I know that it's so. Music is so powerful that it can literally change our moods in a few bars; songs can make us happy or sad or nostalgic or (in the case of old Culture Club ditties) make us want to chip out our eardrums with an ice pick. And sometimes, a song can trigger all four reactions during the course of its pop lifetime. (Anyone humming *Frozen*'s "Let It Go" right about now?)

Why do songs impact us so deeply? Why do notes arranged just so and sung just right make an Italian rapper's eyes well up? I have no idea. Perhaps science will figure it out someday. But I know this: of everything we've talked about in this book, music is perhaps the entertainment world's most powerful conduit to the soul, the most personal expression of emotion and spirituality there is. I think that's why faith and music have been linked from the very beginning.

A whole biblical book is dedicated to psalms, or songs to God—some of them among the book's oldest writings. We're told to "sing to the Lord" upwards of 120 times—*waaaay* more often than we are told to homeschool or put little fish stickers on our cars. "If any of you are suffering, they should pray," we read in James 5:13. "If any of you are happy, they should sing."

When I think about why I believe in a loving God, lots of arguments and discussions and theological dissertations come to mind. But my emotional answer is much simpler: laughter and song. Laughter taps the unbridled joy of creation. Song brushes its glory. These evolutionary non sequiturs help make life worth the living.

In *The Magician's Nephew*, one of the books in C. S. Lewis's beloved *Chronicles of Narnia* series, the lion (and Christ figure) Aslan creates a world by *singing* it into existence. How right that feels.

And when it comes to finding spirituality in music—unlike the movies and television shows we've already discussed—you don't have to look very hard. If God whispers in a superhero flick or hints at something in a television show, it can seem like he positively bellows in song. Faith is right out at the front of the stage, tap dancing in the spotlight, *demanding* our attention. From Gregorian chants to Bach-penned masses to Audio Adrenaline's "The Houseplant Song," Christian music has always been about making a joyful noise. And *noise*, by definition, ain't quiet.

In 2012, CCM and gospel artists sold about 22.9 million albums—more than classical, jazz, and new-age artists *combined*. That same year, both Christian rapper TobyMac and worship artist Chris Tomlin planted albums on the very top of Billboard's Top 200 chart. There's a lot of great and popular (and sometimes both) Christian music out there.

But you don't need a Christian book to tell you that Christian music has Christian messages in it, right? At least I hope not. (Though, if you do, please contact my editor and let her know. She's always on the hunt for new book possibilities.) When you buy a Chris Tomlin album, you're looking for inspirational worship songs, not a kickin' track to twerk to.

But not every Christian musical artist is a *Christian* musical artist, if you get my drift. In fact, many bands made up of Christians don't even like being called a Christian band. They shrink away from the CCM label as if they were Martha Stewart and CCM was a Quarter Pounder wrapped in sequins.

"My life will be judged by my obedience, not my ability to confine my lyrics to this box or that," Switchfoot frontman Jon Foreman said somewhere, which was requoted about a billion times without attribution on the Internet. "We all have a different calling; Switchfoot is trying to be obedient to who we are called to be. We're not trying to be Audio A or U2 or P.O.D. or Bach: We're trying to be Switchfoot. You see, a song that has the words: 'Jesus Christ' is no more or less 'Christian' than an instrumental piece. . . . You see, Jesus didn't die for any of my tunes. So there is no hierarchy of life or songs or occupation only obedience."

If CCM is a musical church, artists and bands such as Switchfoot are more like wandering pilgrims (maybe not wholly unlike Sister Cristina when she wandered onto the very secular stage of *The Voice*). They travel from place to place, from smartphone to smartphone, sharing a song or two and moving on. They're perhaps not out to evangelize, exactly (though if listeners are moved closer to faith through them, they'd probably be gratified). But faith is an integral part of who they are and what they love, and it dances across their music like light on water. They may not claim to be a "Christian" artist or a "Christian" band, and yet the spirit of Christ is, once you see it in their music, impossible to ignore. And because these artists also are incredibly gifted—among the best at what they do in many cases—they're impossible for the secular world to ignore, either.

Do *U* know of a band that might fit the bill? Yeah, me 2.

THEY WILL FOLLOW

The members of a little band named U2 were just getting their hair figured out back in 1981. Sure, they'd already released a well-received (if little-bought) debut album named *Boy*. But by their own admission, they were still working on their craft. They didn't know how to play very well. Their songs seemed to move people not through their lyrics (which were, compared to their later work, fairly juvenile), but through the sheer charismatic willpower of lead singer Bono. Their follow-up effort needed to soar like an eagle—but when a briefcase containing Bono's lyrics for the new album was lost on tour shortly before the band was due to start recording, it looked like the whole venture might crash like a turkey thrown from a helicopter. They went into the studio unprepared, with lead singer Bono occasionally improvising lyrics as they went.

But even as they were working on the album, they were going through another crisis. The band's Christian members—Bono, guitarist The Edge, and drummer Larry Mullen Jr.—were wondering whether rock 'n' roll was compatible with their faith at all.

The threesome belonged to a Christian group called Shalom Fellowship at the time. "The idea was to create a Christian community, where people would live and work under strict Christian standards," Mullen later said in *U2 by U2*. "When you're young and impressionable, it all sounds ideal."

But while U2 was recording all of Bono's impromptu lyrics, according to the *Dangerous Minds* blog, a member of Shalom said he had a prophetic vision that U2 should disband and worship God as God intended—without all the distractions and distortions that come with the rock lifestyle. Pressure for U2 to abandon its music kept building inside the church, and Bono, Mullen Jr., and The Edge wondered if they all had a point. They took a couple of weeks off between concert tours to figure out what to do.

Bono talked over the issue with agent Paul McGuinness, according to the *Irish News*, and McGuinness responded thusly: "God doesn't believe in breaking contracts."

Bono eventually stayed with the band and left Shalom Fellowship, followed by The Edge and Mullen Jr.

"We were getting a lot of people in our ear saying: 'This is impossible, you guys are Christians, you can't be in a band. It's a contradiction and you have to go one way or the other,'" The Edge later told journalist Bill Flanagan for *U2 at the End of the World*. "They said a lot of worse things than that as well. So I just wanted to find out. . . . So I took two weeks. Within a day or two I just knew that all this stuff was (bleep). We were the band. Okay, it's a contradiction for some, but it's a contradiction that I'm able to live with."

The album released during this crisis of faith was called *October*. It's not regarded as one of U2's best. But even in a four-decade career saturated by spirituality, their second album ranks as perhaps U2's most religious. "Gloria," the album's second single, features a Latin chorus that translates to "Glory in you, Lord / Glory, exalt," with nods to verses in Colossians and James. "With a Shout (Jerusalem)" contains such lyrics as "I want to go, to the foot of Mount Zion / To the foot of He who made me see." The band longs for the return of Jesus in "Tomorrow": "Who tore the curtain / And who was it for?"

And on it goes.

With *October*, the band set a trajectory they'd continue to follow throughout their careers. It cemented the fact that U2 wanted to sing about something more than dancing and drinking; more than couples breaking up and making up; more even than socie- tal ills that desperately need correction. They were willing to deal with the last transgression. They were willing to talk about God.

And for their entire careers, they've been willing. Sometimes the songs have been searching and questioning, sometimes ex- ultant in what they've found. "I was born to sing for you," Bono sings in *No Line on the Horizon*'s "Magnificent." "I give you back my voice." In "Breathe," from the same album, we hear that "Ev- ery day I die again, and again I'm reborn"—a line that, for me, perfectly echoes the paradox of my own Christian journey: how I need to set aside the failures of the previous day, ask and accept forgiveness, and be reborn again in God's love.

These guys aren't perfect. Do a search online using "U2" and "Christian," and you'll find a veritable avalanche of articles detail- ing just why the band is horribly apostate. And yet, I'd have a hard time believing that members of the band would spend so much time talking about God if he didn't mean something extra special to them. And I think it's fair to ask whether Bono—one of the world's best-known philanthropists—and the rest of the band would be as involved in charity work without the hand of faith in their lives.

The truth is, The Edge is right: living Christian *and* being in the world's biggest rock band comes with contradiction—a dis- sonance that's hard to dispel. To be a rock star means, on some level, to play the role of a demigod onstage. As Christians, we're called to be humble and deflect praise to the One who made us.

But maybe that dissonance isn't so different from what most of us struggle with in our non–rock star lives. We're selfish when we should be generous. We take when we should give. We don't always walk the walk like we should. We stumble into bad habits and career headlong into temptation. We talk about how God has changed our lives when, sometimes, he feels quite distant, quite silent. Faith is *hard*. And to walk perfectly in God's footsteps is impossible. That doesn't mean that we shouldn't try to weed out the dissonance. But it does mean that we should accept that, in this life, it'll never entirely go away.

"It's very important for Christians to be honest with God," Bono told Focus on the Family President Jim Daly. "God is much more interested in who you are than who you want to be."

GETTING REAL, FEELING RAW

I think that's something that has always attracted me to bands like U2. They are who and what they are. Even back when I discovered them in the mid-1980s—their *The Unforgettable Fire / The Joshua Tree* period—they sounded so unlike anyone I'd heard. They didn't aspire to be the next version of The Who (who did influence them) or the Bee Gees (who did not). They were all about being U2. Say what you want about the band, they've never tried to be anyone or anything else. They've never apologized to the secular world for their spirituality. They've not tried to appease their Christian fans by making a worship album or scrubbing away some of the messiness found in their music. U2—from Bono's wailing vocals to The Edge's searing needlepoint guitar—has always felt honest, eloquent, and strangely raw.

Granted, maybe the band is more duplicitous than I'm aware of. Perhaps, back in 1976, they coolly plotted their conquest of the musical world. "First, Bono, you gotta get a mullet," they might've said. But to me, the band has always felt real. They didn't find a template for cool and follow it. They made their own. And isn't that what we, as Christians, are supposed to do? To be true to ourselves and the God who made us? To use our gifts and celebrate the unique attributes God has given us? Christianity has never been about being cool. It's been about being honest—about our strengths, our failings, our doubts, and our boundless joy in God.

U2 can be messy. And when it comes to faith, I appreciate the mess. My own spirituality has always been a little disheveled, and so I'm always a little envious, and slightly skeptical, of people whose relationship with God feels so *tidy*—those who have a feel-good, doctrinally pure answer for everything. I'm not saying that such people are faking it; I think many have been given, for whatever reason, the gift of easy faith—a wonderful thing for those who've been blessed with it, but a rather confusing condition for those who haven't. I struggle to trust God wholeheartedly like I should. I struggle to see the story he's telling.

When I read the Psalms, I really dig those that belt out praise to God: "I will bless you every day," reads Psalm 145:2. "I will praise your name forever and always." But in my own life, I think I take even greater solace in the psalms that express suffering and anger and even troublesome questions while still remaining deeply faithful to a sometimes confusing Creator.

> God! My God! It's you—
> I search for you!
> My whole being thirsts for you!

My body desires you
in a dry and tired land,
no water anywhere.

(Ps. 63:1)

So while I sing Chris Tomlin songs in church (and really enjoy doing so), I gravitate toward messier music. I listen to the traveling pilgrims.

I listen to the multi-Grammy-winning band Mumford & Sons's meditative "White Blank Page" (from *Sigh No More*) and hear desperately submissive lyrics such as "And can you kneel before the king / And say I'm clean, I'm clean."

I listen to Switchfoot's *Vice Verses* and hear Foreman singing about our shared desire for a transcendent "Blinding Light"—the beauty and glory we feel is the antidote to this fallen, gray world.

I'm still looking for the blinding light
Still looking for the reason why

I listen to Owl City's buoyancy and optimism in almost everything Adam Young writes, and the plea for listeners to be the hands and feet of God, singing,

Here's your one choice to give a helping hand.
There's room at the table for more.

I listen to indie darling Sufjan Stevens, his *Illinois* album heartbreaker "Casimir Pulaski Day," about a friend who dies of cancer the morning of the Chicago-area holiday. And its honesty about faith in the midst of tragedy is both cutting and healing:

All the glory when He took our place
But He took my shoulders and He shook my face

All of these artists deal with Christianity in slightly different ways. Marcus Mumford of Mumford & Sons not only didn't want to be known as part of a Christian band, he even distanced himself from the label of *Christian* itself in a 2013 *Rolling Stone* interview. "I think the word just conjures up all these religious images that I don't really like," he said. "I have my personal views about the person of Jesus and who he was. . . . I've kind of separated myself from the culture of Christianity."

Owl City's Adam Young, on the other hand, embraces the label. Some of his songs mention Jesus more often than some CCM artists have mentioned the name during their whole careers. "My prayer is just that God give me the songs He wants me to sing and that they will be extremely 'usable' by whatever capacity He chooses to use them," he told the *Christian Post* in 2011. "I feel like anything beyond that is almost none of my business!"

The point is, all of these artists have taken inspiration from Jesus. They, like we, have felt that he has something critically important to say. They don't mirror him perfectly, of course. In some cases, their "discipleship," if you could even call it that, is most imperfect, indeed. But that, perhaps, makes them a lot like most of us. We're sometimes angry with God. We wonder what his will really is for our lives. Sometimes, we may wonder whether he listens to us at all. A few of us may even wonder what it really means to be Christian. And yet those of us who call ourselves Christians still love him. We love him with a certain desperate adoration. As Peter told Jesus, where else could we go?

"I think the Good News is about grace and hope and love and a relinquishing of self to God," Sufjan Stevens said in an interview with the *Quietus* in 2010. "And I think the Good News of salvation is kind of relevant to everyone and everything."

CODA

Stevens is right, of course. The good news is, in itself, a kind of music. Sure, the four Gospels—Matthew, Mark, Luke, and John—are the collected stories of Jesus: who he is, what he said, what he did. Together, they're histories in poetry, mysteries with the greatest twist ending ever. But what they represent, the good news itself, is pure song. The gospel is about a love too great for words, a hope beyond imagining. It is a reality that directs our gaze both inward to the pit of our souls, and outward to the vastness of heaven. It is indeed a relinquishing of self, but in so doing we become more ourselves than ever. Through the gospel, we die and yet live. We lose ourselves, and yet we are found.

The gospel is what brings tears to our eyes even as we laugh. It is sunlight in our pocket, a nova in our hands. The gospel makes these artists who they are and sing the praises of someone so much greater. It is the reason for their gifts and the best excuse to use them.

The gospel is the greatest inspiration, the last transgression. The gospel is what makes a young nun sing.

CHAPTER 10
ETHICAL CHOICES IN VIDEO GAMES

To (Take an Arrow to the) Knee, or Not to Knee,
That Is the Question

I'm not a bad guy. I just make bad decisions!
—Henchman, *Batman: Arkham Origins* video game

It's amazing, really, that this book exists at all, considering my ongoing obsession with *The Elder Scrolls V: Skyrim*. I know, I know: by the time you read this, *Skyrim* probably will be ancient history. It was pretty old even when I was writing this chapter. But don't get all judgey on me; there's a lot to do in that thing.

If you aren't familiar with *Skyrim*, you play as a guy (or girl) known as the Dragonborn, a man (or woman) of whom prophecies have been written since the beginning of time about the guy who will off the terrible dragon Alduin, "Eater of Worlds." You also can be, if you so choose, the chilly country's *numero uno* fighter, magician, thief, brawler, werewolf, real-estate mogul, zombie-slayer, sword maker, sweet-roll baker, bunny killer, and about a gazillion other things. If you buy all the gaming add-ons (and I have), you can do even more stuff—get married, have kids, build houses, sail to ash-covered islands for gloomy vacations, you name it.

In one of these add-ons, you are tasked with bringing *Skyrim's* vampire infestation under control. To do this is more involved than just toting around a bunch of garlic (though you'll find lots of that in the game, oddly; I suspect its makers were big Italian food fans). No, you've got to team up with a vampire and talk with her mother in a very gloomy, purplish extradimensional world called the Soul Cairn.

Naturally, it's not just a matter of booking passage to the Cairn, talking with the lady, and high-tailing it back to earth. Nooooooo. The place is dark, oddly colored, and physically toxic, and any living being that steps into it will find his very soul slowly sapped away by the place's horrific energy. (It's a little like a Las Vegas casino, in that.) There are only two ways to get around this literally soul-threatening predicament: you either can store a little of your soul away in a special gem or some such, which'll somehow protect you (working something like an Internet cloud backup, maybe?) but leave you less able to deal with the nasty beasties lurking in the Cairn. Or you could transform into a vampire yourself: vampires, being already dead, don't have a problem with soul drain.

I decided to become a vampire. And as soon as I made my decision public, my twenty-year-old daughter was completely aghast.

"Father!" she cried. "Where are your morals!?"

I felt horrible. Never mind that this is a game where you already kill more fake people than a pixelated petty dictator. Never mind that I would get my desiccated heart a-beating again as quickly as possible. In my daughter's eyes, by becoming a vampire, I was making an unethical decision. Because my character was choosing a dark road, so was I.

CHOICES, CHOICES

Video games have always been about more than just having dexterous thumbs. They've been about making wise choices. In the fledgling days of the genre's history, when the games mostly were found at the corner arcade or the neighborhood pizza joint, those choices were extraordinarily pragmatic: Do I use my thrusters to get away from the asteroid or try to blast the thing? Should I send my pellet-gobbling Pac-Man down this hallway or that one? These decisions were incredibly important—yea, truly life-or-death choices (at least within the context of the game). They were simple, primal choices, similar to what our distant ancestors might've faced when stumbling across a really peevish saber-toothed tiger: we needed to decide, and quickly, what steps we needed to take to keep ourselves from dying. And even though our games digitally gave us the chance to live on *after* death if we had enough game tokens (another important departure from the real world), the threat of pixelated extermination still felt pretty serious in the moment. It's not like quarters or game tokens grew on trees.

But as video games gradually moved from the arcade and into the home in ever-more sophisticated guises, they carried with them an ever-so-slightly greater sense of good and evil too.

Legions of faceless *Space Invaders* or flying *Asteroids* gave way to the in-game boss—from Bowser (most *Mario* games) to Goro (*Mortal Kombat*) to Dracula (*Super Castlevania IV*). These things didn't just kill you: they were *trying* to kill you. They wanted nothing more than to marry the princess and steal your money and embarrass you in front of your friends. BWAHAHA-HAHAHAHA!

And just like that, games became a good versus evil experience. The bosses were obviously the villains. *You* were, by default, the hero—no matter how many mostly innocent underlings you had to kill along the way. It was morality as understood by a two-year-old: you wanted something; a boss was keeping you from it; therefore, the boss must be bad.

But video games have continued to evolve—their storytelling and art growing ever richer and more complex—and so has their sense of morality. And sometimes, in a sense, it's that morality that makes games worth playing.

Remember, we're the sort of people who love a good story. And integral to good stories—most of them, anyway—is a sense of purpose and conflict and reason. If our characters must fight for something, it's got to be something worth fighting *for*. Moreover, we've got to have a sense as to why these legions of adversaries are worth fighting *against*. And both of these motivators— both the carrot of reward and the stick of rampaging zombies or whatnot—are predicated on, in a way, morality. Yes, it's a twisted, often-inconsistent sense of morality at times—an ethical system that might get you arrested, flogged, and executed in most countries. But as imperfect as it might be, there it is—an ethical system that tells you not what to do to get to the next level, but tells you why it's "right" to do it.

In fact, morality is about the only constant that most games have. Even when video games completely obliterate every physical and natural law on the books, the only laws left are those hinged to a vague sense of right and wrong. In *Portal*, players shoot pathways through empty air and hop through an upside-down, topsy-turvy world that'd make even M. C. Escher dizzy. Drop something through a hole in the floor, and it could plummet from the ceiling. Up is down there, unless it's sideways. But right is still right, wrong is still wrong, and we gamers all know better than to trust GLaDOS and her promises of cake.

Even in games where all Ten Commandments are broken constantly, those commandments still mean something. Would law-flaunting satirical games like those in the *Grand Theft Auto* series sell if they didn't? Yes, such games are built on breaking rules—legal, biblical, and otherwise. If *GTA* took place in a world *without* such rules, it would lose its reason for being. Even when you're playing a bad guy, you have to have some sense of what "bad" is. The very paradox might make the whole series vanish in a puff of pixels, never to be seen again.

Video games take place in a universe where at least some aspects of right and wrong are universally understood and shared. And, as we've mentioned before, such a universal understanding of morality points to a staggering assumption: that there's some sort of moral core to the universe itself—something that tells us how we ought to behave. Christians like me call that core God.

C. S. Lewis, in explaining that universal moral law in *Mere Christianity*, says that such a law is difficult to observe: We live, after all, in a world that resembles *Grand Theft Auto* more than we might like. But, he adds,

> we do not merely observe men, we *are* men. In this case we have, so to speak, inside information; we are in the know. And because of that, we know that men find themselves under a moral law, which they did not make, and cannot quite forget even when they try, and which they know they ought to obey.

Games such as *GTA* give us the ability and encouragement to break that moral law. But the game does nothing to refute the existence of such a law. In fact, it rather proves it. Video games may smash the laws of physics, but even they can't escape that sense of morality we share. They can't escape God.

And video game spirituality doesn't stop there. As game designers continue to explore the medium's storytelling possibilities, they're forcing gamers to make moral decisions of their own. It's no longer about survival; it's about just what you're willing to do to survive and win. Will you kill innocents to boost your own power? Will you dally to help a poor, helpless widow defend her homestead? Many games these days want to test how you'll behave. And your in-game future, your happiness, your very virtual salvation might depend upon the choices you make.

THE POWER OF A MOUSE

Disney's much-beloved Nintendo Wii game *Epic Mickey* was one of the first real kids' games to encourage players to think about their in-game decisions.

Granted, players never had to debate as to whether to steal a virtual car and mow down innocent civilians. Given that you're playing as Mickey Mouse, the most venerated Disney character ever, that sort of radical choice making would seem rather extreme. Disney would never let its beloved mouse turn into Scarface (though hearing him peep, "Say hello to my little friend!" would've been pretty great). But still, decisions matter here. And there's even a hint of God overseeing the whole affair.

The story begins with Mickey sneaking into the laboratory of Yen Sid, his old wizarding pal from *Fantasia*. The wizard's been making a new world for "things that have been forgotten." But when Mr. Sid leaves the room, Mickey decides to play around with the master's paint and paint thinner—accidentally creating a fearsome Shadow Blot that dives into this now-thoroughly stained and thinned world.

All this, by the way, has some great parallels to the Genesis story of Adam and Eve. They, like Mickey, kinda messed up their own world through their sneaky meddling. They, like Mickey, ran and hid from the deed initially, hoping the whole thing would maybe just blow over (or at least that God wouldn't blame *them* for it). But eventually they, like Mickey, are forced to deal with the mess they've made.

In *Epic Mickey*, our large-eared protagonist must fix the world through the prodigious use of paint and thinner. Paint creates things in this world and attracts pleasant-looking bubble-like guardians called Tints. Thinner obviously destroys stuff and attracts Turps. And while you need to use both paint and thinner to get through the game, the thinner is sort of a necessary evil; use too much thinner, and the characters around Mickey will look as if their dogs had just died that morning. They mope and sigh. Some slouch. And while the thinner-loving Turps that surround Mickey are helpful in a pinch (they'll make some bad guys disappear on contact), they're clearly not the sort of entities to which you'd want to give a big hug. Not if you're made of paint yourself, anyway.

Using paint, on the other hand, fills characters with joy. They'll sing. Sometimes they'll twirl around in happiness. The Tints, instead of destroying bad guys, will turn them into Mickey's friends. And here's an interesting kicker: they work way better on the biggest, baddest bad guys than the Turps do. According to *Epic Mickey*, Paul was right: love never fails.

In the midst of all this painting and thinning, the mouse can go on ancillary quests to help his fellow 'toons . . . or not. And while Mickey never breaks all the way bad in this game, the character's actions do impact what gamers will see at the end. Choices matter, *Epic Mickey* tells us. Our decisions not only impact us, they also impact the world around us.

"Be the change you wish to see in the world," someone who wasn't Gandhi (sorry, Instagrammers) once said. The Bible tells us to look to the needs of our neighbors too. "Instead of each person watching out for their own good, watch out for what is better for others," Paul says in Philippians 2:4. "But if a person has material possessions and sees a brother or sister in need and that person doesn't care—how can the love of God remain in him?" John asks in 1 John 3:17.

Not a bad lesson from a little mouse, is it?

DROWNING IN CHOICES

Epic Mickey wasn't the first game to introduce morality-based decision-making into its world, and it's far from unique.

In the *Fable* games, you are peppered with moral decisions that can have a huge impact on gameplay. In *Fable II*, you might even sprout a halo or a pair of horns. *Fable III*'s character morphings don't go quite that far (though you can grow wings), but your morality—whether you break promises or not, or whether you're willing to sacrifice for the nice folks of the kingdom—still has a huge impact on how you look, how happy your country is, and even what your dog looks like. It's as if the game's makers read Galatians 6:9: "Let's not get tired of doing good, because in time we'll have a harvest if we don't give up." They just fast-forwarded to the "due season" a bit.

The post-apocalyptic *Fallout* games, most noticeably *Fallout 3*, measure your "karma." If you do good stuff—everything from saving innocent people to making someone feel better about their weight—you get karmic points. If you decide to slaughter your friends or kick puppies, your karmic level dips. And while karma is, of course, a concept out of Eastern spirituality, the symbols they use to tell gamers their karmic level are strictly Christian. If you're doing good, karmically speaking, you'll see a little angel avatar. Do great, and you'll see Jesus himself—bedecked in a robe and crown of thorns. If you're a bad, bad person—prone to lying and cheating and eating corpses—your little karmic indicator will sprout horns and a tail and carry a pitchfork. Sure, the game requires you to engage in a whole bunch of rather un-Christlike actions—the game does not encourage you to turn the other cheek when faced with weapons-toting mutants, for instance; but through its little karmic symbols, *Fallout 3* suggests that Paul was on to something when he said, "Follow my example, just like I follow Christ's" (1 Cor. 11:1).

One of the most interesting manifestations of video game morality, I think, takes place in the original *BioShock*. Players, slipping into the virtual skin of protagonist Jack, are thrust into an underwater dystopia called Rapture—a one-time capitalist retreat that's gone very, very bad. Most of the remaining residents are violently bonkers, and to make your way through the game you've got to collect stuff called EVE (a substance that allows you to use lots of nifty bioweapons) and ADAM (gunk that sparks certain mutations that make you more powerful). ADAM is particularly important in the game: the more you get, the better off you are, tactically speaking. But there are a couple of catches: One, the stuff is addictive as anything, and ADAM is what made Rapture's residents go nuts to begin with. And two, ADAM resides in innocent kids called Little Sisters. If you help free a Little Sister, you'll get a little ADAM to help you on your soggy dystopian journey. But if you kill her, you'll get a whole lot more. And just like that, you're faced with an ethical conundrum: Should you go the easy route, kill the Little Sisters and play simply to win? Or travel the harder path and save some Little Sisters along the way?

Now, let's step out of the biosphere and look at the wider, religious metaphorical landscape of *BioShock* for a minute. Consider: Rapture was intended to be a paradise of sorts—a new start, an Eden, as it were, unspoiled by the fallen world topside. And ADAM and EVE are obvious allusions to *the* Adam and Eve. But in *BioShock*, the substances represent not our naked friends, but rather the forbidden fruit: each substance was fortified with forbidden power that would make the citizens of Rapture more (as a certain evil snake might say) like gods. And while that wasn't a lie, exactly, it triggered the fall of this promising world, and its residents were banished into Loopyville. It's all an M-rated echo of Genesis, really.

This is the environment in which our main character finds himself—a leaky Eden. He cannot escape the sin of this strange world. But in saving Little Sisters one by one, Jack can bring a measure of salvation to the world as a whole. Or he could just try to accumulate all the ADAM he can, using whatever means necessary.

Which way is better? We know which way Jesus would suggest. "Go in through the narrow gate," he says in Matthew. "The gate that leads to destruction is broad and the road wide, so many people enter through it. But the gate that leads to life is narrow and the road difficult, so few people find it" (7:13-14). As for the game itself—well, you can "win" using both techniques. But

BioShock's finale is wildly different depending on how much of a jerk you were.

Take the ADAM forcefully, and you win as a monster. We are told that the surviving Little Sisters "offered you everything, yes? And in return, you gave them what you always did: Brutality." We see you, as Jack, ferociously shake a Sister, then proceed to spread violence and bloodshed not just in Rapture, but in the world at large. Eden, it seems, is lost forever, replaced by this (your) dark iron vision.

But take the gentler path, and we see a different ending. When the Little Sisters offered up Rapture, we are told that Jack did "what I've come to expect of you," according to the narrator. "You saved them. You gave them the one thing that was stolen from them: A chance." The final cut scene tells us that Jack turned down the city and took the Sisters up to the surface, becoming a surrogate father to them. They went to school. Got married. And as you slowly passed away of old age, they surrounded you, holding your hand in theirs.

"In the end, what was your reward?" the narrator goes on. "You never said it, but I think I know: a family."

It's a great parallel, really. Because while Jack would make a very poor Christ figure in most ways, this act of sacrifice has some nice parallels to our own Savior. After all, Jesus could've been an earthly king too, had he listened to Satan. But instead, he gave himself to us to give us a chance—a chance to forsake our own ruinous city of sin and live as God intended us to. We don't have to accept that chance, of course. But as the Little Sisters figured out, it'd be kinda silly for us not to.

A MORAL CONUNDRUM

Game designers don't just wedge in a bunch of morality to point the way to Jesus, of course, or even to make players better people. Without being told, we already know (thanks to that universal sense of morality we discussed earlier) that killing innocent girls for mutant juice is probably not the best way to behave in real life. But these choices do make games even more immersive than they already are. These games don't just engage our minds and thumbs anymore; they touch our hearts and souls.

"I think players simply get tired of experiencing the same things over and over and over in games," Emil Pagliarulo, lead designer for *Fallout 3*, told *Gamespot*. "Frankly, it gets boring. When morality's involved, the simple act of shooting a bad guy isn't so simple anymore. You've got to ask yourself, 'Well, is he really the bad guy? Was he maybe just trying to defend himself? Should I really be doing this?' So just the act of questioning what you've done a thousand times before instantly makes it different, and more interesting, and therefore, in a lot of cases, more fun."

Not everyone agrees with that assessment. Some point to the inherently simplistic morality found in these games. Sometimes, the morality has no real impact on the storyline. In others, making a certain ethical decision will lock you out of parts of the game. Even in *BioShock*, the "narrow gate" isn't all that narrow. Sure, you get less ADAM from the Little Sisters if you save them. But every once in a while, the game rewards you with extra ADAM for being such a good guy—thus making your sacrifice not so sacrificial at all.

Some gamers believe that morality is inherently different in the world of video games, so to wring our hands over one Little Sister when we've already become Rapture's most notorious killing machine seems a little inconsistent.

They've got a point, of course. I'm the sort of guy who can't even smash a spider in the real world; if one should visit, I gather it up in a glass and gently usher it outside. But that hasn't kept me from killing men, beasts, dragons, and all manner of things in *Skyrim*. Part of the charm of games in general is that they give us a chance to act in ways that we wouldn't ordinarily act. We can become superheroes or race car drivers or mafia hitmen. And when you're a gamer like I am, you often don't think that much about it.

And yet, a sense of morality tethers me to the real world. While I can dispatch digital villains without too much angst, I never killed a Little Sister in *BioShock*. I don't think I could. Even though I know they're really just a collection of code crafted by a handful of game makers somewhere, extinguishing that code is a step I won't take.

That can make games such as *Skyrim* feel, for someone like me, like a two-hundred-hour morality play.

FINDING LIFE AMONG THE DEATHLORDS

Skyrim's own morality engine is more open-ended than some. While the game is absolutely saturated with ethical conundrums, they have little bearing on your gameplay. Oh, sure, you'll get arrested if you get caught stealing or killing a city blacksmith, but you can pay a bribe or fine and get out of that easily enough. And should an evil godlike being ask you to sacrifice a guileless follower to them? Well, instead of a rap on the hand, you'll be rewarded with a special suit of armor. Your only real punishment is the imagined disapproval of *Skyrim*'s virtual citizens and whatever's going on in that cold, cold heart of yours. Frankly, if you don't make some moral compromises in the game, you'll miss the chance to play some of it.

But maybe, just maybe, this makes *Skyrim*'s system of morality the most realistic of them all.

Sin, after all, has a certain appeal. It can be fun. It can be rewarding. Sin wouldn't be able to tempt a turnip if it didn't offer us *some* sort of satisfaction. Sin opens "doors" too: We won't know the experience of meth unless we try it. We'll never know what it's like to have an affair unless we actually have one. And while lots of sins have built-in societal and legal consequences, sometimes the only thing that stands in the way of our sinning is . . . well, us.

The Bible warns us that the real world can feel a lot like *Skyrim* sometimes. "They repay me evil for good, / hatred in return for my love," Psalm 109:5 tells us. In fact, the Psalms are full of cranky reminders that the world isn't always fair. Sometimes, the evil guy gets the new suit of armor. The rewards of being good can feel a little less tangible sometimes.

And yet there are rewards. In going through that narrow gate, we hopefully help those around us. We set an example of fair play. We mirror God a little better to the people around us. And we hold truer to, again, the eternal and universal sense of right and wrong, of good and evil, to which even video games must inherently submit.

Even in *Skyrim*, this digital land of bad behavior, we are re-minded of those universal morals. We're reminded that, if we are really the hero of this story, we've got to act heroically.

"The All-Maker made you Dragonborn for a higher purpose," Skyrim's heroes are told at one point. "Do not forget that." Some-times, in this virtual world of violence and temptation, it's hard to remember—just as it is in the real one. But it's important. And it has its own reward.

I haven't always made the most righteous decisions in *Skyrim*. I did feel pretty guilty, for instance, about the whole vampire ep-isode. And your good deeds, even if you end up saving the world from that bad beastie Alduin, don't wash away your bad choices. Salvation through works, no matter how great and powerful you are, never does the job.

Skyrim reminds me that morality is not something we can choose to define. It was defined for us, long ago. Morality comes from a moral Creator, and we have not the power to change his definition of it, even if we are the Dragonborn.

And it makes me ever more grateful for God's literally saving grace—that we are saved. Our sins, virtual or real, can be erased through his forgiveness. I'm so grateful that even video-game vampires have a chance at redemption.

CHAPTER 11

A STILL, SMALL VOICE

Finding God's Fingerprints in the Stories You Love
(or at Least Watch)

It's like in the great stories, Mr. Frodo. The ones that really mattered. Full of darkness and danger, they were. And sometimes you didn't want to know the end. Because how could the end be happy? How could the world go back to the way it was when so much bad had happened? But in the end, it's only a passing thing, this shadow. Even darkness must pass. A new day will come. And when the sun shines it will shine out the clearer. Those were the stories that stayed with you. That meant something, even if you were too small to understand why. But I think, Mr. Frodo, I do understand. I know now. Folk in those stories had lots of chances of turning back, only they didn't. They kept going. Because they were holding on to something.

—Samwise Gamgee (Sean Astin), *The Lord of the Rings: The Two Towers*

To **believe in God is to be human,** studies suggest. There are people who reject that belief, of course, but the instinct to believe seems hardwired inside us. About 85 percent of us worldwide adhere to some sort of religion. About 92 percent of us believe in God, according to a 2007 Pew Research study. So pervasive is the belief that even 22 percent of self-professed atheists and 55 percent of agnostics believe in a higher power. Researchers have found that kids, even kids raised in faith-free households, believe that the world was designed and that most everything in it has a purpose. We humans are amazingly adept at looking at the world around us and being able to discern purpose and meaning behind all the mess.

That ability is, I think, one of the big reasons why we humans got so civilized in the first place: we saw the order behind the chaos and believed, in our very core, that we had an important place in that order. We developed sciences to better understand the world and the hands behind it. We developed governments to help bring a greater sense of logic and fairness to our own little microcosms, reflecting the greater purpose around us. We developed the arts to express our wonder and terror and confusion with it all. In the beginning, none of our creations were designed so much to glorify us but to glorify God.

Ironically, some will say that instinct to believe is itself a product of the chaos—an evolutionary instinct that helped us cope with a strange, cold, and soulless universe.

But I don't think that's true. God created us because he loved us, and we're told he wanted us to love him back. It seems so logical, then, that he would've designed us with the desire to seek and see him, don't you think? And when we earnestly look for God, we can't help but find him—sometimes in even the most unexpected places.

It's been that way from the beginning, really: God was in the rain and rainbow in the story of Noah. He was in Jacob's dream and Joseph's jail. He was in Egypt's plagues and Jericho's walls. He could be found in Assyria and Babylon and Rome as well, working through his followers and sometimes using his naysayers to further this glorious story of ours. He doesn't make people do bad things, I don't think—we do that just fine on our own, thanks very much—but he can take that bad and turn it into something good, take the mess and make it beautiful.

And God's still doing that today. We see his fingerprints in nature and science. We see his influence in our friends and family.

Our church, as imperfect as it sometimes is, can still feel alive with his presence. And he works in our art too—not just our explicitly Christian movies and songs, but in the secular stuff as well.

I'm luckier than most. Over the last several years, I've had the opportunity to watch movies and television, listen to music, and play a few games through an explicitly Christian lens. Part of the purpose is, of course, to warn discerning Christians from stuff that might shock their sensibilities and not explicitly glorify God. That's a really important aspect of the gig, and I do think there's an inherent friction between Christianity and crass entertainment. "More than anything you guard, protect your mind," we are told in Proverbs 4:23, "for life flows from it." Paul, in Philippians 4:8, says, "From now on, brothers and sisters, if anything is excellent and if anything is admirable, focus your thoughts on these things: all that is true, all that is holy, all that is just, all that is pure, all that is lovely, and all that is worthy of praise."

But when you think a little deeper, it wasn't like Paul was living in a particularly lovely, commendable, or praiseworthy world. There was no system of Christian colleges or home schools to keep impressionable youngsters away from the wiles of the Roman Empire, no Christian music to drown out the clanging of the pagan bells, no Christian business directories to keep Christians safe from Jupiter-worshiping bakers. Paul's world was not just messy, its secular influence also was pervasive. There was no getting away from it.

And so I sometimes wonder whether Paul wasn't asking us to hide from the wider world as much as he was imploring us to live with integrity in the midst of it. We can't lock ourselves away from the mess. But maybe, with God's help, we can find God's beauty and truth in the midst of it. As I have tried to do in this book.

It's not like you need to be a trained professional to do this, by the way. Sure, if you want me to tutor you on how to tally f-words in movies, just drop me a line and we'll talk. But sussing out some good, redemptive messages can be pretty easy, I think, if you go into the exercise with an open heart and your brain fully engaged. God may be whispering, but he's still speaking a language we can understand. He's not a peevish Latin teacher, after all.

So with all that said, let me give you a window into some of the things I keep in mind when searching for God's fingerprints in what I watch or listen to or play.

BE AWARE OF YOUR OWN WEAKNESSES (AND STAY AWAY FROM ENTERTAINMENT THAT EXPLOITS THEM)

This is incredibly important: it's really hard to concentrate on God when you've got a particularly comely man or woman posing suggestively in front of you on the movie screen. Temptation may seem old-fashioned, but I think it can still throw some pretty serious walls between us and our Creator, even in the movies.

In my work for *Plugged In*, we note anything we feel might be an issue for someone: sex, violence, language, projectile vomiting, you name it. Sometimes it's a matter of sensitivity or squeamishness: not all of our readers think that, say, fart jokes are all that funny. But often, it's because problematic content can serve as triggers in our minds and souls. We know how corrosive pornography can be to real, flesh-and-blood relationships, and sexual content in movies can be just as damaging. Listening to foul language in music can normalize profanity, making it more likely the user might swear like an uninhibited Yosemite Sam.

But the sneaky truth is that not all of these content issues impact everyone the same way. An example: I haven't used a swear word in context for fifteen or twenty years or so, and it's not like watching *Dallas Buyers Club* would give me the urge to start swearing up a storm. Profanity is just not something I struggle with.

In fact, my biggest problem isn't something that fits into a "negative content" box at all. While stray nudity doesn't trigger lots of impure thoughts, puppy-dog teen romances can throw me for a loop. Crazy, huh? They tend to make me overly nostalgic for high school—a time full of hand-holding passing periods and kissy-wissy dances, and refreshingly free of mortgages and onerous book deadlines. I feel wistful and, more important, *old* when I watch those sorts of movies. And if I didn't try to check and ameliorate these emotions, I might one day run out and buy a Corvette just to make myself feel better.

Not all of us have a great handle on what issues we might have. We all have weaknesses that we have trouble seeing. You may tell yourself that watching a violent movie has very little impact on your soul . . . and then the next thing you know, you're shaking your goldfish angrily, saying, "Don't stare at me like that, you little punk!"

The point is, if you think a movie or an album or a game either might disgust you or tempt you, then stay away. No bit of entertainment, no matter how many Oscars it's won or how many of your friends are talking about it, is worth it. Corvettes can be very expensive.

FORGET ABOUT FINDING PERFECTION

We said at the very beginning that there's no such thing as a perfect story or a perfect God-honoring work of art. We live in a fallen world, and everything we touch has a bit of corruption clinging to it. When you insist that a work of fiction or art or music must be without flaw to contain a little burning bush in it, you'll be looking for a long, long time.

I'm bound to get a lot of angry letters about this book, and I understand why. Almost everything I've mentioned in this book has some very, very obvious flaws. About 80 percent of the stuff I've talked about here wouldn't get a thumbs-up from *Plugged In*, nor should it. And please, don't take anything written here as an endorsement of any given bit of entertainment. Don't cue up *Breaking Bad* on your Netflix account just because it's a great depiction of the corruption of sin.

But that also doesn't change the fact that it is a great depiction of what sin and our own excuse making can do to us. Don't assume that, just because something has its problems, that it doesn't also have its merits. If you're going to engage with stuff that isn't wholly true or beautiful, try at least to see the true and beautiful that might be found within. God's fingerprints sometimes can be found on our messiest works. His burning bush can illuminate some dark places. Don't try to squeeze our Creator into a box and presume to tell him where he can or should speak.

He's God. He does what he wants. He speaks how he wishes. And again, if he's willing to talk through Balaam's donkey or a flaming shrubbery, I think God can speak through our very imperfect stories.

KNOW YOUR BIBLE

If you want to know what God might be telling us now, it's good to know what he has told us before.

This is particularly true when it comes to stories. God knows, I think, that sometimes we need to be told the same thing over and over before we really get it.

The story of Jesus' death and resurrection is maybe the most obvious example. It's a story that most of us are pretty intimately aware of, and we can see echoes of it in loads of modern-day tales. Aslan sacrifices himself for a wayward little boy in *The Lion, The Witch and the Wardrobe*. Little Ofelia gives up her own earthly life to protect her little brother in *Pan's Labryinth*. It's hard to name a superhero movie that *doesn't* feature the hero holding his life loosely. The list of sacrificial movie heroes runs into the hundreds, if not thousands.

Very few of these stories, of course, are necessarily conscious reflections of Jesus' own world-changing work. But that doesn't stop the echo of the Greatest Story. It doesn't negate God's fingerprints. And when we're familiar with the stories that we've already been told in the Bible—or in other Christian works too, for that matter—we are able to detect similar motifs and ripples through these new stories we are told.

But it doesn't stop with the stories, of course. The Bible's overall themes of love and grace are important as well. Movies often quote or allude to Bible verses too, and a little familiarity with them can enrich and bring new power to a narrative. In 2010's *Secretariat*, about the famed Triple Crown–winning racehorse, we hear a beautiful passage from Job 39: "Do you give the horse its strength or clothe its neck with a flowing mane?" it begins (v. 19). The verses lay some surprisingly spiritual cobblestones for this beast-based biopic: with the table so set, we see Secretariat not as just a racehorse, but as one of God's most beautiful, most stunning creations. And when Secretariat runs, we can almost feel God's joy.

And then there's the flip side of that: had I been a little more familiar with the book when I saw *Pulp Fiction*, I would've known that Samuel L. Jackson's "righteous man" biblical quotation was taken almost entirely not from Ezekiel, but from the book of 1 Tarantino.

ENGAGE YOUR BRAIN AND PRAY

This is something I do before every movie and television show I watch—pray that God will help me to see what he wants me to see, protect me from what I *have* to see, and, no matter what, be with me throughout.

I'm not sure how such prayers "work," of course. Prayer, for me, has always been a mysterious process. After all, God already knows what I need from him without my asking (though the Bible does tell us that he likes to be asked). I sometimes wonder whether God puts such an emphasis on prayer because he knows that the mere act of praying will help us just as much.

I don't know what God does with my prayers. But I know how they benefit me. I find that prayer helps focus my attention and energy on what I'm watching. No longer am I watching simply to be entertained or moved or shocked, but to be pushed into a higher sense of awareness, really. It helps me both distance myself from some of the problematic content and, paradoxically, makes me more sensitive to some of the movie's underlying subtext— what the moviemakers are trying to tell us, and what messages the film itself might unintentionally be conveying.

I think prayer is really important not just in discerning entertainment, but in everything we do. When we pray, not only are we doing what God repeatedly has asked us to do, it also reminds us of something incredibly important: we are not of this world. We don't belong to it. We belong to Someone greater than than the world, higher than it. I need to remind myself of that quite often, I've found. If I don't, I'm prone to drift, I think. It's easy to drift into a sort of zombie state—to forget that God gave us new life, and that we don't have to be satisfied with the old one.

But whether you take the time to pray or not, never go into any bit of entertainment with a brain that's not fully engaged. It's important to think about what you see and listen to and not let it just wash over you. Bring your whole being into the theater and watch actively, not passively. Don't allow assertions to go mentally unchallenged or emotional moments to pass by unexamined.

Hey, you paid good money to see this thing, right? You might as well get your money's worth. You shouldn't take an intellectual nap through it.

TALK, TALK, TALK

After an advance movie screening, there are often studio representatives waiting for me at the door. "What did you think?" they'll invariably ask. Usually I'm able to give them a word or two. But in truth, a lot of times, I don't quite know what I thought of a movie right away. Sometimes, I don't even know whether I enjoyed it or not. It took me three days to coherently decide that Terrence Malick's *The Tree of Life* was a work of genius.

I like to chew on a movie for a while. Digest it. I live a ways away from most of my movie screenings, and the ninety-minute drive gives me a little time to think about what I've seen. I turn the themes over in my head. I think about some of what the characters said and did. I mull over the movie's apparent worldview and where God would have fit into it all.

And whenever I have a chance, I talk it through with some people.

I'm amazed at how much this can help. Even after I have mentally sorted through a movie or whatnot—after I feel like I've examined every inch of the thing and feel like I "get" it—it's amazing how much a five-minute conversation either can bring more subtext to the surface or make you feel like, hey, you had the whole thing all wrong. If you can talk with someone who took something entirely different away from a movie, all the better; I kinda liked *Noah*, but talking about it with some folks who hated it was an incredibly stimulating and, I think, healthy exercise for all of us.

And that's not the only place I get a little intellectual confirmation or pushback. After I write a review, it's pretty fascinating to see what another critic, Christian or not, might've pulled out of the very same movie. Sometimes *Plugged In* readers will offer insights, through e-mail or a blog response, that had not even occurred to me. There are some very smart people watching movies these days—you are likely one of them—and I think that we can all gain insight from the folks around us.

Again, the key is not simply to watch (or listen or play) and forget. Think. Mull. Discuss. Even if you don't pull out a fantastically memorable spiritual message, you're surely going to become a better movie watcher that way. Why, you might even become a movie snob and wonder why I didn't once mention *Cinema Paradiso*!

CONVERSATION STARTERS

'Course, talking through entertainment on a spiritual level doesn't always come naturally to any of us. We'd rather talk about how cool the car chase was or how much we enjoyed the talking dog or how simply amazing it is that Patrick Stewart never seems to age. So with that in mind, here are a few questions that might get you thinking, and talking, a little more deeply about the films you are watching, the shows you are seeing, and the games you're playing. And, not so coincidentally, they nicely gel with the themes we've talked about in this book. Not all of these questions will pertain to every movie. If you are watching a movie like *The Hangover*, maybe none of them will have any pertinence to your search. But hey, until *Burning Bush 2.1* comes out, this'll have to do.

1. Do you see people acting sacrificially? Giving of themselves to help others? Who? Why? Are they rewarded
   for this?

2. What's the movie's central crisis? How do the characters
   face the challenge? Does it feel like it could be the end of
   the world? What sort of hope are the characters holding
   on to? Is it a realistic hope? Why or why not?

3. What monsters are in the picture? Why are they frightening? Are they natural? Supernatural? Do they represent any real-world issues we suffer today? How do our
   heroes deal with them?

4. Are there people who are walking around as if they
   were—metaphorically or literally—the walking dead?
   Do they have any hope of coming back to life again?
   What sort of threat do they pose to the living? Do they, at
   times, mirror those who are living? If so, in what ways?

5. What have our heroes and other characters lost? What
   impact have those losses had upon them? How do the
   characters move on? Do they find new hope? New life?
   And if so, how do they find it?

6. When you look at a story's hero or heroes, what are
   their strengths? What are their weaknesses? How do
   those weaknesses impair them? Do they overcome
   those weaknesses? If so, how? If not, what do you think
   stopped them?

7. How do the decisions our characters make impact our story? Does one bad choice mess things up for everybody? Does one good choice help make everything better? Do you see people making the right choices for the wrong reasons? The wrong choices for the right reasons? Explain in some detail.

8. Is God an explicit part of the story? Is he a force for good? How do you think the main characters view God?

9. Are there people of faith in the story? What sort of faith? Are they good people? Bad? Comic relief?

10. What message do you think the filmmaker wants you to take away from this movie? Or is he or she just happy you bought a ticket?

11. Can you see God's fingerprints on this film? When? Where? How?

As you might've guessed, we have reached the end of this book. This is the point where I wish you a happily ever after and type THE END, preferably as violin-heavy exit music plays in the background.

But as I mentioned about 190 pages ago, the best stories never end. And while this book has come to its merciful conclusion, the story behind it—your story, the story of our entertainment, and the glorious story God authors behind it and through it all—is still being written.

  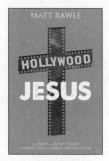
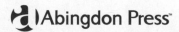